THE HALF-ACRE HOMESTEAD

46 YEARS OF BUILDING & GARDENING

Lloyd Kahn & Lesley Creed

THE HALF-ACRE HOMESTEAD

46 YEARS OF BUILDING & GARDENING

Lloyd Kahn & Lesley Creed

Shelter
Publications

Distributed in the United States by Publishers Group West and in Canada by Publishers Group Canada

Library of Congress Control Number: 2019952167

6 5 4 — 25 24
(Lowest digits indicate number and year of latest printing.)

Printed in China

Note: A 50-page PDF on design considerations, small buildings, and stud-frame construction from *Shelter II* is available free at **shltr.net/shelter2-excerpt**.

Shelter Publications
An imprint of AdventureKEEN
2204 1st Ave. S., Suite 102
Birmingham, AL 35233
(800) 678-7006; fax (877) 374-9016

Email: shelter@shelterpub.com

Shelter's Website: www.shelterpub.com
Lloyd on Instagram: www.instagram.com/lloyd.kahn
Lloyd's Blog: www.lloydkahn.com

Shelter
Publications

Contents

Introduction

When Lesley and I first got together, it was homesteading at first sight.

We both wanted to create a home and grow our own food. I'd been working as a carpenter for about 10 years and had built a homestead in Big Sur in the '60s *(see p. 158)*. Lesley had been gardening, sewing, and practicing crafts most of her life.

We both wanted to do as much for ourselves as possible. We both wanted to avoid paying rent or getting a bank loan. And we both wanted to have a home built of natural materials, and that was functional, practical, and good-feeling.

21st-century homestead When I say "homestead," I don't refer to the original meaning of the word as it applied to farmers claiming land in America in the mid-1800s.

Ours is a homestead in the sense of building our own home and growing much of our own food on a (small) piece of land.

Starting We began in 1974. We had a 100′ by 200′ lot on the Northern California coast — about half an acre. (To give you an idea of the area, a football field is roughly an acre in size.)

Here's the story of our adventures in providing our own shelter, food, and practicing crafts on this land. There are also lists of useful tools. And it's a look at what we see in our everyday life, inside and outside the house.

We've learned a lot by trial and error, and want to share our experiences with others who are interested in *homemade* and *handmade* shelter, food, and crafts.

Skill level Our building, gardening, and cooking skills are not on the professional level. I'm an owner-builder, not a highly skilled carpenter. Lesley's cooking is simple and delicious, not fancy. Her garden is home-oriented, not professionally landscaped. The tables I've made are crude by cabinet makers' standards; I think of them as folk art. The point is, these are things you can accomplish on a do-it-yourself basis without getting hung up by the absence of perfection.

The '60s and the '70s It's said that the '60s happened in the '70s"; that's only partially true. The '60s happened in the '60s *and* the '70s. Much of what we did in the '70s was inspired by the some of the counter-cultural concepts of the earlier decade, which we both arrived at independently. *(See brief notes on the '60s on p. 154.)*

Reinventing the wheel In the '60s, there was — among some of us — a spirit of relearning skills of the past. Building one's own home, growing vegetables (and preserving the surplus), managing chickens, bees, and goats, making bread — skills that had been abandoned by our parents' or grandparents' generations.

It's a juggling act — there was always more to do than time to do it. We didn't take holidays. We mostly stayed home and kept busy — enjoying the process as well as the results.

There were maybe 35 of us building our own homes in or on the outskirts of our small town in the '70s. It was probably amusing to the older inhabitants here to see a sudden influx of young people learning skills and crafts that previous generations had given up.

Easy living This was possible then because it was a time of great prosperity in America. You could live on very little money and take the time to experiment, try things out, learn new skills. Land was cheap (ours was $6,500), and building codes, planning codes, and fees were reasonable rather than onerous, as they are today.

Self-sufficiency It's important to realize that self-sufficiency — like perfection — is a *direction*. You never get there. No one is completely self-sufficient. Nothing is perfect.

You can't grow all your own food. You probably can't do every bit of house building yourself. The point is to do as much for yourself as possible.

Handmade: A few things haven't really changed much from 40 years ago. A computer is not going to build your house for you, nor plant your food (nor make quilts or shawls). These things still need to be done with human hands. Just about everything you see in these pages was done by hand.

Analog times The bulk of our house building was done before computers. Much of what we learned came from books. It was truly a different world. We communicated with landline phones (when possible) and letters via the U.S. Post Office. *The Whole Earth Catalog* was immensely useful for a large group of like-minded people.

There was no Facebook, no Instagram, Apple, Google, Alexa, or Amazon. There was no internet!

If you wanted to build a house nowadays, what if you took all the time you now spend in the digital world (well, a lot of it), and spent it building? Just sayin.'

Assembling this book I'm the communicator (blabbermouth) of the family. From an early age, I've written about, talked about, taken photos, blogged, Instagrammed, and published books about what I run across in the world. The same here. Most of the text here is in my first-person voice.

But as I've watched this book develop, I've realized that, although I'm doing most of the writing here, these pages are a testament to Lesley's creative skills,

her arts and crafts. She's the captain of this ship, and the food, the garden, the flowers, the quilts, the way things look and work around here is all her doing.

Could you do this nowadays? Times are way different now than they were when we did the bulk of this work.

You could do some of the things we've done here without devoting as much time to these pursuits as we have. You could scale it back compared to what we've done. This book is descriptive, not prescriptive.

For example, you could remodel an old house instead of starting from scratch. If you live in the city, you could grow parsley on your fire escape, bake bread, buy fresh ingredients at farmers' markets. You could remodel your living space, build some of your own furniture, do your own maintenance, make your own repairs.

For more on the possibilities of small-scale homesteading these days, see "Could You Do This Nowadays?" p. 153.

The benefits In the last few years, we've looked around and thought, "This is pretty good."

The house has been upgraded, changed, remodeled, and is working well. The kitchen is a far cry from the outdoor kitchen with washtub sink that we started with. The soil in the garden is black and rich from decades of improvement. The chicken coop is working well (in its fifth incarnation). Every day we make improvements, do necessary maintenance, and tune things up.

We have no mortgage. We pay no rent. We live in a place that we love, that we've crafted and created with our own hands, that is ever evolving. This is our handmade world.

The House

In the early '70s, I had just come off a five-year period of building geodesic domes (a friend of mine called it "circle madness"), and had concluded that they didn't work — for a variety of reasons.* Before that, I had built post-and-beam houses. Nothing as simple as stud-frame construction, which I discovered in 1971. Eureka! Rectangles!

Notes on Design

After years of experimental building, I realized that building a home shouldn't be a "trip," at least not for me. A dome, a 7-sided building, a sculptural design — building a home from an abstract idea — is not sensible for most people, in my opinion. It's going to take much longer, and cost a lot more money.

Our aims We started relearning skills that had been abandoned by our parents and grandparents. We felt that modern life had lost touch with the practicalities. We felt that homes being designed by architects had nothing to do with the kind of life we wanted to lead.

We wanted a home with versatile, useful space, a place to cook, eat, get warm at night, to sleep, to heal, to listen to music and sit around the table and talk, where we'd be able to work on projects, dry clothes on a rack, put up guests comfortably, and have the necessary practicalities (water, heat, kitchen, lighting, plumbing, etc.) functioning well. We wanted it to be built of materials that felt good to be around, to be colorful, and to have good *Feng Shui*.

---

*I published two books on dome building before giving up on domes. For a more complete account, see **www.shelterpub.com/domes**.

Designing during construction We designed as we went along. First the kitchen and bathroom, then an expansion of the living space. At first we had an old, wood-fired cook stove that heated our main room and on which we did some cooking.

In those days, a lot of builders made a departure from the typical house, in which kitchen, dining room, and bedrooms were all separate. They opted for an open floor plan — cooking, eating, and sleeping all in the same room, often with an open loft. As time went by, people wanted more privacy, so they started partitioning off the bedroom(s).

Building 45 Years Ago

Building a house back then was way different from now:

1. Tools: There were no portable drills, no grabbers (construction screws), no chop saws, no laser transits, no portable planers or joiners.
2. Insulation: There wasn't much choice — certainly no insulation that was non-toxic in its manufacture.
3. Greywater systems weren't in use.
4. There were no insulated windows.
5. Solar water heating and generation of electricity were in their early stages of development.

Construction I won't go into detail about building the house, other than that the main part of it was stud-frame, and built largely of recycled materials — wood, windows, and doors. There's a very thorough section on building a stud frame house in *Shelter II* that is available free online at **shltr.net/shelter-2**.

The earliest part of construction is what I like best. The foundation, floor framing, and then — nailing down the subfloor, my favorite part of the building process. Creating a floor where there was nothing but space and now standing on it. It's a great feeling.

I can get a building framed, sheathed, plumbed, and wired, but I'm not good at the details: the finish work. Over the years, I've had a succession of carpenters help me tune things up.

What We'd Do Now

I sometimes fantasize about building another house — we've learned so much, there are so many things we would do differently. But since that's most likely not going to happen, we've written up our ideas now, with all these years of experience and trying things out, as described on pp. 150–151.

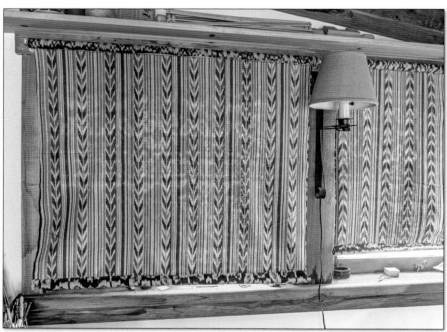

Roller blinds *Lesley ordered custom lengths of rollers and flats from a local blind shop, then attached the heavy fabric. At the base, she sewed in the flats, which are ⅜″ by ⅞″.*

Crocheted wool blanket
by Elisabeth Kirkland

"So many books,
so little time."
  –Frank Zappa

Building — then living in — a home is like an instrument you're constantly tuning, or a book you are continually rewriting. It's a process that's never over.

Working on this book has been an intensive experience in introspection. I've looked at what we've done here with more than usual interest and seen the trial-and-error evolution of the house and garden — living and breathing entities — the flows, patterns, and operation of the whole.

Dining Area

Dining area, breakfast nook
Remodeling of the room by Michael
Gaspers and Franz Skinner. Windows
made by Franz out of redwood water
tank staves that Michael had salvaged.
Flooring by Jan Broek.
  We put out birdseed on the ground
and there are always a multitude
of birds to watch. We can also keep
an eye on the chicken coop. I built
the table out of salvaged Douglas fir
3×12s.

Heating

Wood heat This Vermont Castings soapstone wood stove has provided our main heat for over 40 years. It's a wonderful tool, made in America, built to last. The slabs of soapstone absorb and store the heat, then radiate it into the room for hours.

All our firewood comes from trees knocked down in storms that I find on the roads. It's mostly oak or bay, and some eucalyptus. I cut it up with a chain saw, bring it home, and then once a year, rent a log splitter. It's fun to scout the roads for fallen-down trees.

After splitting, it's stacked to dry for 6 months to one year.

Kindling

Kindling is from scrap lumber; I seem to have an endless supply of short pieces or rotted wood, which I cut to size (about 16″) on my radial arm saw, then split with a hatchet.

We use these bags to carry firewood and kindling into the house from the woodshed.

The wood stove heats the main living room and kitchen in winter. The bedroom and bathroom are not heated. We have two windows open all year in the bedroom for fresh air, and keep warm on cold nights with a down comforter.

Electric heat In the studio, we use a couple of 660-watt (very low wattage for an electric heater) Zell Aire infrared radiant ceramic heaters. (I don't believe they make this brand any more.)

We don't use them for space heating as much as we use them close by wherever we're working. When I come out to the office on a cold morning, I'll turn on one that's about two feet away from where I work at my computer for maybe an hour, and then turn it off; it continues to radiate heat from its ceramic panel for a good while.

In my mind these are the best type of electric heaters, especially compared to higher-wattage, fan-driven heaters, which produce a dry heat.

Layering This is an important, simple, and much-overlooked method of keeping warm. In winter, I'll sometimes have on five layers: cotton, merino wool (Icebreaker and SmartWool brands especially), fingerless gloves, down jackets in various combinations, homemade wool scarves, and knitted wool hats. (Heat the person, not the space.)

Window Drapes

Loose curtains
I cut 1½″ dowels to length, make brackets out of short pieces of used wood, attach dowel holders to them with screws, and Lesley makes the curtains, which we hang from the wooden rings. She uses heavy material that provides some measure of insulation, and blocks light when closed.

Roller blinds

Skylights

In all our various buildings, we have more than a dozen very simple skylights, using double-walled polycarbonate greenhouse panels. This is a very strong plastic similar to Plexiglas, guaranteed for 10 years (although some of ours are still fine after 15 years). They provide 80 percent light transmission and a measure of insulation. (*See p. 104 for use of these panels in our greenhouse.*)

The panels are cut to size and slipped into the roofing material like a big shingle. The method is pretty foolproof, but I would bet they're not legal under current building codes.

They provide a lot of light, save on electricity, and are especially welcome on cold, overcast days.

You can get these panels at Tap Plastics, or shipped from Farmtek, a great source of greenhouse and agricultural products in Iowa: ***www.farmtek.com***

Insulation

I used aluminum-backed fiberglass batting because it was the only viable option 40 years ago. I didn't want to use polyurethane foam for a variety of reasons. These days, there are a number of non-toxic insulation materials available, such as recycled denim, sheeps' wool, hemp products, or soybean foam.

Heat loss I averaged things out in various reports to the following: In an *uninsulated* stud-frame house, 30 to 35 percent of heat is lost through the roof, 21 to 31 percent through the windows, and 18 to 25 percent through the walls. The remainder of heat loss is through the floor and air circulation.

Production studio shows built-up skylight on shallow roof at right, and three simple shingle-style skylights at left.

Shingle-type skylights on shop

Septic System

There are over 25 million homes in North America utilizing septic systems. They are in areas where there are no sewers. The process is called "onsite wastewater disposal," and it means that wastewater is treated adjacent to the home.

It's a simple and highly ecological system, and the systems generally work so well that homeowners are hardly aware of the process going on.

The conventional (non hi-tech) septic system is powered by gravity. No motors. If functioning properly, wastes are treated and purified by microorganisms in the soil. A marvelous system.

I built my first septic system in Big Sur in the '60s. It consisted of a 600-gallon circular tank and a leach field with pipe and gravel. It was a do-it-yourself kit, consisting of lightweight, semi-circular concrete blocks and a concrete top. I laid the blocks with mortar, made a tank bottom with several sacks of readymix concrete, slid the top on, had a backhoe dig the trench, installed pipe and gravel, and *voilà* — wastewater disposal.

The system is still working, I hear from the present owners of the house, over 50 years later.

For our present house, I had a 1000-gallon septic tank with adjacent drainfield installed 47 years ago, for about $3,000, and with periodic inspections and occasional pumping out of solids, it has worked fine to this day.

The miracle of gravity-fed septic systems is that no power is used in the process of wastewater disposal.

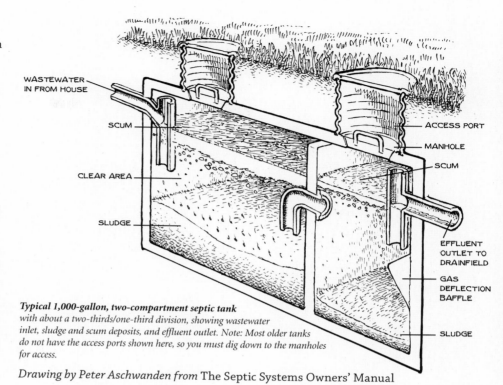

Typical 1,000-gallon, two-compartment septic tank
with about a two-thirds/one-third division, showing wastewater inlet, sludge and scum deposits, and effluent outlet. Note: Most older tanks do not have the access ports shown here, so you must dig down to the manholes for access.

Drawing by Peter Aschwanden from The Septic Systems Owners' Manual

I became fascinated with septic systems in the '90s, and ended up writing *The Septic Systems Owners' Manual*, which explains what a septic system is, how to maintain it, and what to do if things go wrong. (Drawings for the book were done by Peter Aschwanden, the illustrator of John Muir's *How to Keep Your Volkswagen Alive: The Idiot's Guide*). If you have a septic system — and pardon what the Car Talk guys called "shameless commerce" — I highly recommend this book. You can save yourself a lot of grief if you understand the process going on and how to inspect and maintain your system.

Note: While working on the septic book, I discovered what is in effect a plot against gravity-fed septic systems. Engineers and inspectors have colluded in much of the country to require homeowners to install complex septic systems (such as mounds) that are expensive, (in fact) ecologically destructive, and often unnecessary. (The more expensive the system, the higher the engineering fees and the permits, which is fine with the engineers and regulators.) In 2014, I testified before the Ohio senate in Columbus, Ohio, about corruption in the American septic industry. Don't get me started!

I wrote an article in *The Mother Earth News* in 2008, titled "The Truth About Septic Systems," viewable at **shltr.net/septicmother**.

Wood-Heated Sauna

I built a small (6′ by 9′) sauna in the '90s. It's well insulated and lined with cedar. The benches are redwood with counter-sunk screws; you don't want to be sitting on a hot screw head.

There's a small wood stove with rocks on the top for absorbing heat. The jug is for pouring water on the rocks to make steam. Taking a sauna is a great way to detoxify; the skin is the body's largest organ of detoxification.

Solar-Heated Outdoor Shower

It couldn't be simpler: basically a black box with a tank and double-walled poly-carbonate glazing, built by Dan Conroy of Grass Valley, California. It's worked perfectly for over 20 years, with one replacement of the glazing plastic. No moving parts.

This water heater is the simplest and cheapest form of solar water heating (sometimes called a breadbox heater). I never take a shower in the house. The water is warm even on foggy days. It's rusted out at one spot along the bottom of the box, but this doesn't affect its operation.

Each time I take a shower, I'm both amazed and grateful to have the hot water coming from the sun. Somehow, it *feels* different (as opposed to fossil-fuel–heated water).

Solar-heated outdoor shower

Solar Electricity

In 2015, we had a 5.23 KW photovoltaic solar system installed (by American Solar) that provides most of the electricity for our home and office. It consists of 16 32″ by 62″ Sunpower 327 W panels. We installed new roofing under the panels. The electricity is fed into the PGE grid via an SMA Sunny Boy 6000 inverter.

It's a great thing to see PGE bills where we're generating more electricity than we're using — especially since it's powering not just our home, but our publishing operation — a half-dozen Mac computers, copy machines, printers, and other office equipment.

Curved-Roof Shed

In researching and eventually publishing a book on tiny homes, I came to the conclusion that a curved roof, as with *vardos* or gypsy wagons, practically eliminates the feeling of claustrophobia that is common in tiny spaces.

I believe that the prototype steep gable-roofed tiny home, with a loft and ladder, is a bad design, and that the *vardo*, with the bed at one end and drawers underneath provides a much more comfortable space.

I hadn't built anything for years, and decided to build a small shed with a curved roof. There are several ways to achieve curved rafters and I decided to make them with laminated bender boards.

I got 16´-long, ¼˝-thick by 4˝-wide rough redwood bender boards and laminated four of them together for each rafter. I nailed down a piece of scrap lumber for the central point, bent the boards and held them in place with diagonally opposing studs.

I applied Titebond wood glue with a paint brush and clamped them together about every foot. It took a while, as I could only make one at a time, and had to let each laminated rafter set up for 24 hours.

The building is 10´ by 10´. If I did it over, I'd probably make it 10´ by 12´ or 10´ by 14´, so it would be rectangular rather than square.

Billy Cummings helped with the project; in fact, he did most of the work, including cutting out the curved double-wall polycarbonate upper windows at each end.

We used salvaged 1×4 tongue-and-groove flooring from Heritage Salvage in Petaluma. For the corner studs, I pieced together short pieces of driftwood 2×4s; the other studs are new.

Glazing above doors is cut from double-wall polycarbonate greenhouse roof panel.

Bender boards glued and clamped

Bender board rafters, sheathed with 6´ redwood 1×8 fence boards

The roof sheathing is 6´-long, 1×6 redwood fencing from Home Depot. The roofing is red roll roofing. Insulation in the walls is Ultra Touch recycled denim.

Exterior sheathing is ⅜˝ rough-sawn Douglas fir plywood. Recycled windows and the two doors are from Urban Ore in Berkeley and the interior sheathing was milled out of 4´-long cedar staves from an old hot tub that a neighbor was throwing out.

There's a deck, and the bed is on wheels so it can be wheeled outside on fog-free nights to sleep under the stars.

Conclusion here: It takes a lot longer to do a roof like this as opposed to, say, a shed roof, but once done, it's a lovely space.

Interior wall paneling:
Resawn cedar staves
from recycled hot tub

L–R: Lloyd and Billy Cummings

Exterior sheathing: ¼″ resawn cedar plywood

The Kitchen
The Heart of the House

Our first kitchen was outdoors, on a deck, with a corrugated fiberglass roof. We cooked out there for several months while I was building the house. We used a camping stove for cooking and a galvanized washtub for a kitchen sink, draining through a hose into the garden.

We slept in a tiny temporary room I built, about 8′ by 10′, just enough room for a bed and little black and white TV.

We wanted a kitchen that could be used for many jobs: making bread and noodles, canning, making jam and beer, and a multitude of other things.

Lesley prepares most of our food —all of our own (sourdough) bread, for example. She makes sushi, gnocchi, pasta, tacos, and dozens of other dishes from scratch.

We've always bought in bulk, especially whole grains: wheat, brown rice, and oats. (*See Pantry, pp. 30–31.*)

We moved into the house and used the kitchen I built for maybe 10 years, until Lew Lewandowski did a complete kitchen remodel.

Lew is a meticulous carpenter. He installed the used stainless-steel sink, designed and fabricated a unique dish rack (which is as useful now, 25 years later, as it was then), built Corian counters and cabinets and drawers.

I'm not a highly skilled carpenter. I built the foundation and did the framing, and then had carpenter/friends do the finish work. Lew also remodeled our bathroom. Michael and Franz enlarged our breakfast nook, complete with custom windows (using redwood from a salvaged water tank). (*See pp. 14–15.*)

Left: BlueStar Range. A life changer. No electronic controls or screen. For oven convection, you turn on the fan. It's such an upgrade from 25 years of a Jenn-Air. Many cooks prefer it to the Wolf Range. When you remove one of the four ring grates, there's a well and about a two-inch space down to the burners; a wok nestles down so no wok ring is needed. Both the burners and oven work better than any stove we've ever used. It's easy to clean. Made in America. A wonderful tool.

Note: There are a lot of compromises in the house due to building it in bits and pieces, over the years, without a comprehensive overall plan from the beginning. A lot of things here could be more efficient. It all makes me want to build one more house, and put into practice many of the practical and efficient design components that I've learned about.

Washing Dishes

I installed a 5-gallon electric hot water heater under the sink, prompted by the fact that's it's a long way from our gas water heater to the sink.

I prefer to have hot water heated by natural gas or propane (or solar panels or wood heat), where the heat is provided directly to the water, as opposed to electrically heated water, when a lot of the energy is lost in transmission from distant power plants. This little water heater doesn't use much electricity and doesn't run a lot of cold water to get to the hot; here, the hot water comes after a cup or two of cold water.

The key component of our dishwashing process is the use of a Rubbermaid dishpan. When we had goats, I installed a dishwasher. But over the years, I realized we were scraping and sometimes rinsing dishes (to keep food particles out of the septic system), semi-washing them before putting them in the dishwasher. Also, it used a lot of power and water. I took it out.

The two other key features of this dish-washing method:

1. Baking soda, which we buy in bulk and use in this container:

   It's a non-toxic product that cuts grease (glasses sparkle) and it can also be used as a deodorant in the refrigerator. It's a natural alternative to Comet or Bon Ami.

2. Rubber scraper:

   Used to scrape all particles of food off dishes and pots and pans (mostly to be fed to the chickens). This is an extremely important process if you have a septic system — keeping oil, grease, and food scraps out of the tank.

Most kitchen sinks have a stainless steel ring anchoring the sink to the kitchen counter — a bad design, which over time often produces rot around the ring (unless the counters are impervious material, like granite or Corian). With this sink, the drain boards slope toward the sink so that water flows seamlessly from the counters to the drain. *(See drawing at right).*

After washing dishes in the dishpan, we rinse and stack them in the built-in dish rack *(above),* where they stay until used again. Usually we'll throw the dish-water out into the garden after washing.

This is all shown in a video here: ***shltr.net/dishwashing***

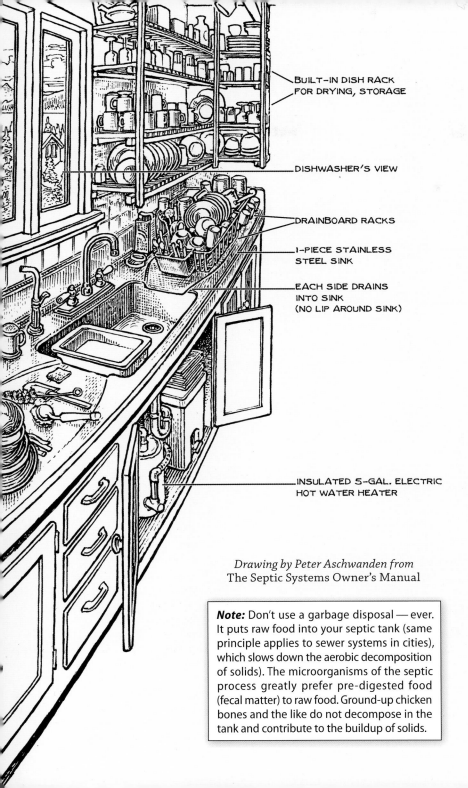

BUILT-IN DISH RACK
FOR DRYING, STORAGE

DISHWASHER'S VIEW

DRAINBOARD RACKS

1-PIECE STAINLESS
STEEL SINK

EACH SIDE DRAINS
INTO SINK
(NO LIP AROUND SINK)

INSULATED 5-GAL. ELECTRIC
HOT WATER HEATER

Drawing by Peter Aschwanden from
The Septic Systems Owner's Manual

Note: Don't use a garbage disposal — ever. It puts raw food into your septic tank (same principle applies to sewer systems in cities), which slows down the aerobic decomposition of solids). The microorganisms of the septic process greatly prefer pre-digested food (fecal matter) to raw food. Ground-up chicken bones and the like do not decompose in the tank and contribute to the buildup of solids.

Composting Food Scraps in the Kitchen

The two main components are:

- The small container for food scraps that we give to the chickens.

- The larger, foot-operated trashcan for all food waste that the chickens won't eat (coffee grounds, avocado pits, orange peels, etc.) We also pour in water from cooking potatoes, rice, and vegetables, all of which have a lot of nutrients.

We give the contents of the small bucket to the chickens every day or two, and I incorporate contents of the other can into the compost pile about once a week.

Thus, all food scraps from over 40 years has gone back into the soil. (*See composting details on p. 85.*)

The Pantry

The pantry was a main part of the design of the house. We wanted to cook as much as we could from scratch, and this meant buying in bulk.

I built the pantry when we were milking goats. A concrete floor to keep things cool and a two-compartment, commercial stainless-steel sink for washing milk buckets and bottles. An adjacent room with outside ventilation through screens for grain and other foodstuff storage. We live about an hour from a main shopping area, so we stock up on basics and store them in the pantry.

Kitchen Tools
Utensils

We are showing certain kitchen tools and utensils here, the ones we feel may not be so obvious. We're not showing our eggbeater or garlic press, but rather utensils we feel are unique in their usefulness, and maybe not so well known.

Cordless Electric Kettle

Chef's Choice 685 International Deluxe Cordless Electric Teakettle

I'm not a fan of cooking with electricity, but this is one electric appliance that we use 3 to 4 times a day, every day of the year. It heats water to tea or coffee (or hot water bottle) temperature in a flash. Our first one lasted maybe six years and we replaced it. While waiting for the new one, it was a drag to wait for the kettle to boil on the gas stove.

shltr.net/hah1

Blendtec Blender

By midday, I'm usually rolling with my writing or book layout and don't like to take the time to make a decent lunch.

Enter the Blendtec and "green smoothies." I put in water, some milk, fresh or frozen fruit, vitamins, protein powder, almonds, hemp, etc. Then I wander in the garden and pick raw greens — parsley (which is fragrant in a drink), kale, chard, or lettuce, whatever looks good, then turn on the Blendtec and have a delicious drink while working.

There are tons of recipes for green smoothies. I use Gold Standard vanilla whey protein — good flavor, high protein (something like 55 grams in two scoops).

This is a big powerful machine and it can be used for any number of things. It's nothing like the blenders most of us are familiar with. In addition to smoothies, you can chop, juice, grind grain, and make soup or ice cream.

www.blendtec.com

Stick Blender

Cuisinart Smart Stick Hand Blender

If you've ever had hot soup fly around the kitchen when trying to blend it, you would love a stick blender. It smoothly blends soup directly in the pot it's being cooked in easily and quickly; also, the whisk attachment is handy for whipping cream and blending smooth custards, etc.

From Cuisinart:
shltr.net/handblender

Grain Mill

WonderMill Model #WM2000

For 30 years, we had an electric, stone-ground flour mill. It finally gave out and I got a steel-grind mill, and it's great. I realize that stone-ground is a better way to grind grains, but the new mill is 20 times faster.

We are grinding most of our own flour for bread. We grind organic California short-grain brown rice for cream-of-rice cereal. Easy to cook, delicious (a little butter, dark sugar, milk), and it's a meal of freshly ground whole grains. We also use it to grind whole oats (called groats) into flour to make sourdough pancakes. No wheat. They're delicious, and thanks to the sourdough, chewy. Fresh-ground whole grains. Easy to do.

www.thewondermill.com

Grain Flaker

Marcato Marga Mulino Flaker

This elegant little Italian grain grinder has three hardened steel rollers that flatten grain for making flakes or cracks it for making hot cereal or granola. I'd never had fresh oats before until my friend Bruno Atkey showed me this device, just after he gave me a breakfast bowl of fresh oatmeal along with flax seeds, shredded coconut, a little hemp oil for flavor, and brown sugar.

When you grind oats, you're taking the whole oat grain (groat), and crushing and flaking it just before you cook it. You get nutty, delicious oatmeal, the flavor of the whole grain just released. The grinder clamps to any surface up to two inches thick. From Pleasant Hill Grain in Nebraska:

shltr.net/grainflaker

KitchenAid

KitchenAid Professional 600

We didn't use the KitchenAid mixer very much until Lesley found a space to keep it permanently on the counter. It's greatly improved her bread making. Hand-kneading for 15 minutes was not as productive as five minutes with the dough hook. There are other tools, such as attachments for whipping cream and egg whites, for making cookie or cake dough, making pasta noodles, even for grinding meat.

www.kitchenaid.com

In Praise of Copper

Over the years, we have accumulated a number of copper saucepans and frying pans. Yes, they are expensive, but they are also wonderful (and they can be passed down to future generations). They are said to conduct heat five times better than iron, and up to 20 times better than stainless steel. (Google **copper cookware** to see a list of qualities.) We use them every day.

Instant-Read Thermometer

Superfast Thermapen #3 thermometer

This vastly improved our preparation of chicken, beef, lamb, and other meats (though we continue to reduce the amounts we eat). Since the advent of these thermometers, many recipes are now giving a temperature for breads, puddings, cakes, and so on.

shltr.net/hah2

Breadboard

A large, rectangular breadboard (probably maple) has served for all our bread/pizza/roll making. We don't even wash it — we give it a good scrape with a steel dough scraper and it carries wild yeast from batch to batch.

Kiwi Knives

These knives are amazingly sharp and amazingly cheap. We use the large one for preparing just about any food. About $15 for the set of three, from The Wok Shop (in San Francisco, on Grant Avenue); check out all their cleavers and knives here.

shltr.net/knives

Accusharp Knife Sharpener

Another simple kitchen tool. Inexpensive, quick, easy to use. It results in a bit of a rough edge, but this can be smoothed with a honing or sharpening steel.

shltr.net/hah3

Pizza Screen

Our friend Amleto, a pizza chef (*pizzaiolo*), gave us two of these about 10 years ago, and we've used them for pizza ever since. You slide the pizza onto the screen, then place it on top of the pizza stone in the oven. Air circulates underneath, and the pizza bottom is crisp and doesn't stick to the stone.

Kitchen Shears

Due Signi Maniago #2C 946/25

It's embarrassing, but over a four-year period, I used four different poultry shears. We have always had a flock of chickens, and when they quit laying, they are dispatched for chicken stew. None of the shears were strong enough to cut their bones (way denser than commercial chicken bones).

I got these from the Italian manufacturer, Due Cigni, and they work very well:

www.duecignicutlery.it

Vintage Wine Opener

Made by a blacksmith. There must be over 100 wine openers out there, in a wide variety of designs, but I bought this because I liked its looks. About a year after I bought it I decided to give it a try, and — *voilà* — it worked fine.

Stock Pot

Vollrath 18-Quart (4½-gallon) Stock Pot

We got this at a professional kitchen supply store. We use it for cooking crabs, canning, soup stock, etc.

shltr.net/hah4

Weber Genesis Gas Grill

Model E310

We've had this for maybe 10 years. We cook all meat and some fish on it. Propane in 5-gallon containers. It's a high-quality product. A few years ago, the automatic sparker/starter stopped working and I got replacement parts from Weber, along with clear instructions for making the repairs. Weber is a good outfit to deal with. Home Depot is probably the best place to get them; I got mine on sale there.

Info on Weber's website:
shltr.net/gasgrill

Butter Spreader

Simple, but immensely useful for spreading butter, cream cheese, jam, honey, mayo, etc. The serrated edges allow you to cut toast after spreading butter on it.

shltr.net/hah5

Cooking
Cooking from Scratch

Lesley: We always knew we wanted to grow food and cook our own, so we designed our house with a large kitchen and a pantry *(see pp. 30–31)* for food storage.

In the '60s and '70s, there weren't many health food stores, specialist suppliers, bread makers, bakeries, or health-conscious restaurants in our area (or anywhere in the U.S., for that matter), so we gravitated towards making the foods we liked from scratch.

San Francisco has always had ethnic neighborhoods and restaurants. Italian, Chinese, Japanese, Mexican, Russian, etc. These restaurants were always part of the mix and an inspiration for what we started doing.

It's funny really. I can't say why we wanted to make things for ourselves. I suppose it was because we knew it to be healthful, cheaper — and delicious!

Cooking from the Garden

Cooking with the season's bounty and out of the garden were things that many of us learned in the '60s and '70s — after the post–World War II era of frozen foods (TV dinners, etc.) — when "easy/cheap/fast" were the watchwords.

Sometimes it seemed as if we were relearning things that our grandparents had practiced, and that our parents had abandoned.

Even with our small vegetable garden, there are almost always vegetables for dinner. Our California coastal climate lends itself to many vegetables being grown year-round.

So we have been working together for over 40 years, and have learned many of our crafts from books. When we couldn't find something in a book, we'd try it out (sometimes over and over!) until we got it right.

Organic: To Be or Not to Be

Lloyd: In 1965, my friend Seth Wingate gave me a jar of organic raspberry jam, and I was hooked. It was delicious. It *tasted* different.

The debate that goes on about organic food generally weighs the higher cost *vs.* the health benefits. Is it really healthier? Is it worth more?

The trouble with testing is that it doesn't consider the *cumulative* benefits of eating chemicalized food. Sure, the rats in the test labs don't die from eating commercially farmed corn, but what about their livers? Is it possible that ingesting apples that have been sprayed causes just a little bit of bodily damage? And that this all accumulates over the years?

Then, there's the effect on soil. Soil farmed organically is higher in fertility, nutrients, and beneficial wildlife. Also, organic farms do not expose farm workers to insecticides or other chemicals.

Finally, what gets overlooked in the debate on organic food is the *taste*. A sun-ripened tomato *vs.* a bland commercially farmed tomato. Organic strawberries, apples, peaches. If you're in doubt, take the taste test.

Pretty much all of our food is organic, and as fresh as possible.

Organic food was hard to find in the Bay Area until Fred Rohe opened Sunset Health Foods in San Francisco

in 1965; he then changed the name to New Age Natural Foods. He had bins of grains, beans, and fresh flour, honey in bulk, nuts by the pound. (There was very little produce.)

I believe it was the prototype for new health food stores across the U.S.A. He then opened a natural foods supermarket in Palo Alto in 1970, which featured a delicatessen counter. This setup was probably the prototype for Whole Foods, which opened its first store in Austin in 1980.

Bread

Lloyd: One of the interesting things about working on this book is that it's made me think about everything we're doing around here. Bread, for instance.

I realized that for the past five years or so, Lesley has been making sourdough bread. We seldom buy bread. Sourdough is a living culture, and she's using the same starter she created five years ago.

Lesley: I made whole wheat bread for some years, using Baker's yeast, and kneading it for 10 minutes or so. This got to be tiresome, and I lapsed for a while until I "rediscovered" bread made with a sourdough starter five years ago.

We'd had a KitchenAid mixer for some years, but the big difference was when I decided to park it permanently on the counter, and not have to haul it out each time I made bread.

For flour, I use a mixture of 50 percent winter wheat and rye, freshly ground in our grinder, along with 50 percent good-quality, commercial unbleached flour.

Sourdough is an easy and forgiving process that fits easily into the day's schedule — with bags of dough for more bread or pizza crust a little later in the week kept in the refrigerator.

To begin, I used Joe Ortiz' book, *The Village Baker,* and made my own starter, inoculated by the wild yeast and lactobacilli found in our kitchen.

A typical schedule: I mix up the starter, water, and flour the night before. In the morning I put the jar of starter in the refrigerator, and mix up more flour, salt, and a little yeast in the mixer — a slow knead for five minutes, then I let it rise for an hour or so in the bowl. This is when I might put some in the refrigerator for another day. Then I form it into loaves or rolls and let them rise on baking sheets sprinkled with cornmeal. (A cooler, slower rise gives the bread or rolls more flavor.)

Then they are baked at around 400° for 20 or so minutes until done.

Pizza

Lesley takes bread dough (sourdough), and fashions it into thin 10″ or so rounds — which then go to each of us to make our own pizza.

There are thousands of pizza recipes out there. It's a simple dish — dough, tomatoes, cheese, and whatever — that lends itself to trial and error and experimentation. Over the years, we've refined it to what works for us. It's fun!

In addition to the ingredients listed in the captions, all of the pizzas have olive oil. They are all cooked in the oven at as high a temperature as possible (500°+), on top of a pizza screen (*see p. 35*), which is on top of a pizza stone.

Mozzarella, sausage, zucchini

Mozzarella, fresh porcinis, fresh cherry tomatoes

Fresh tomatoes, fresh porcinis, mozzarella, anchovies, basil

Fresh tomatoes, mozzarella, fresh chanterelle mushrooms, zucchini

Tomato sauce, mozzarella, sausage, mushrooms

Fresh tomatoes, mozzarella, basil, anchovies

Fresh tomatoes, dried porcinis, mozzarella, watercress

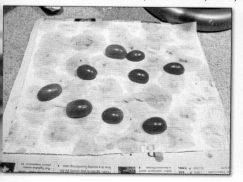

The difficulty in using fresh tomatoes is the water content, which can can make crusts soggy. Roma tomatoes are best. Here, we cut and salted Romas and put them on paper towels (on top of newspapers) to draw out water.

Sushi

Lesley used the book Sushi, *by Mia Detrick to learn how to make sushi rolls. The orange you see on the rolls at right is tobiko, or flying fish eggs.*

Clam Fritters *Three stages shown: (1) Chopped-up (Cuisinart) horseneck clam necks, (2) dipped in egg and cracker crumbs, (3) fried in hot oil.*

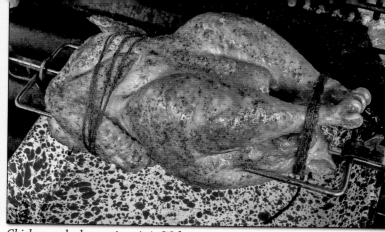

Birds *A duck that caught fire in the Weber. I forgot to put a pan underneath it, and flames leapt high. (It was really good.)*

Chicken cooked on rotisserie in Weber

Oat Waffles

Made with 100% oat flour freshly ground in our mill (see p. 33). Buttermilk, eggs, and little amounts of sugar, baking powder, and baking soda. No oil; no wheat. Wonderful flavor. Maceo and Niko, our grandsons, are fans.

Zucchini Pancakes

Summertime special when zucchinis are overwhelming the garden. We make them like potato pancakes, substituting shredded zucchini for potatoes. With onions, eggs ,and flour, topped with sour cream, along with Pink Pearl applesauce.

Minimizing Bacon Fat

We have bacon maybe once a month, and broil it in a pan so fat drips through, then drain pieces on a paper towel on top of newspapers.

43

Desserts

Homemade fun! (Lesley cuts down sugar to about a third in these recipes.)

Chocolate soufflé
(when we have a surplus of eggs):
Fannie Farmer Cookbook

Bread pudding: *Fannie Farmer Cookbook*

Pecan cinnamon rolls: *The KitchenAid Cookbook*

Trifle, two steps: *Family recipe*

Lemon meringue pie: *Fannie Farmer Cookbook*

Apple custard tart: *Abby Mandell's Cuisinart Classroom*

Bread pudding: *Fannie Farmer Cookbook*

Pecan cinnamon rolls: *The KitchenAid Cookbook*

Preserving Food
Canning

Mostly jam and jellies. We have tons of wild blackberries each summer, a large stand of raspberries, a plum tree, and small patches of red currants and black currants. Lesley makes marmalade from our Meyer lemons.

Fermenting

The small book *Wild Fermentation*, by Sandor Katz, got me interested in fermented food, which has almost magical health benefits. Also inspiring was the wonderful shop, Cultured, in Berkeley, with its selection of sauerkraut, other pickled vegetables, and kombucha tea.

www.culturedpickleshop.com

Sauerkraut I started out making sauerkraut in a 10-liter fermenting crock (with a water seal), but this was too big a batch, so recently I got a water-sealed, two-liter crock, which seems to be just the right size.

shltr.net/hah6

Or, you can get fermentation locks for wide-mouthed Mason jars:

shltr.net/hah7

Olives Until recently, my brother had a farm in the Napa Valley with 2,000 olive trees, and each year I would pick a couple of 5-gallon buckets of olives and use salt and vinegar to cure them. Stored in a container on the concrete floor in the pantry, they last for a couple of years.

Pickled onions

Pickling

This is *so* simple. David Chang's Momofuku recipe for vinegar pickles (or carrots, onions, just about any vegetables): just warm water, a little sugar and salt, and rice vinegar.

shltr.net/pickle

Smoking and Brining Salmon

There are lots of recipes for smoking salmon. For electric smokers, I'd recommend the Cuisinart COS 330 Electric Smoker…

shltr.net/hah8

…and looking up recipes online. I've read that the "biggest mistake in smoking salmon is overcooking." Or check out one of the propane smokers. Or, build your own wood smoker.

But for simplicity in preserving salmon, try making lox. It's just salt, sugar, and a couple of days in the refrigerator. You can look up recipes online. You can then freeze portions of it.

Drying

We've had a wooden food dryer with ten shelves for over 30 years. We used to dry apples and sometimes peaches and apricots, but these days I use it mainly for drying porcini and candy cap mushrooms.

Dried porcinis

Onions drying in greenhouse

Cookbooks

Lesley: My first cookbook was the *Fannie Farmer Cookbook*. I liked her idea of cooking from scratch. Originally published in 1896, it was the first cookbook in America to standardize measurements. Before that, cookbooks would specify "a pinch of salt," "a teacup of milk," etc. It had traditional recipes and I would frequently thumb through it first.

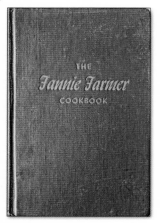

Later, I learned about cooking with the seasons when I discovered *The Art of Simple Food* by Alice Waters, which greatly improved my food preparation. The book elevates simple cooking to an art.

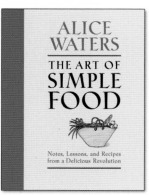

As someone who enjoys the home arts and tends to be an "armchair traveler," I enjoy reading cookbooks. Here is a list of those that I've found the most useful over the years:*

- *The Forgotten Skills of Cooking: The Time-Honored Ways Are the Best* by Darina Allen

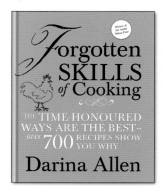

The title says it all. Recipes grounded in country living and the bounty of possibilities.

- *Italian Farmhouse Cookbook* by Susan Herman Loomis

One of those books that is a joy to read; it's like a visit to Italy, with easy ideas to incorporate.

- *Pasta Tecnica* by Daniel Stevens

Italian enthusiasm for all things pasta.

- *Honey from a Weed: Fasting and Feasting in Tuscany, Catalonia, the Cyclades and Apulia* by Patience Grey

A beautifully written account of growing, cooking, and preserving the staple foods of the Mediterranean.

- *Poor Cook* by Susan Campbell and Caroline Conran

One of our first cookbooks, with simple recipes — with the idea that eating cheaply can be simple and delicious.

- *Clearly Delicious* by Elizabeth Lander Ortiz

An illustrated guide to preserving, pickling, and bottling. Great photos, good instructions for preserving the abundance of summer. Especially good marmalade recipe.

- *Salt, Fat, Acid, Heat: Mastering the Elements of Good Cooking,* written by Samin Nosrat, illustrated by Wendy MacNaughton

Wonderfully written, beautifully illustrated, the most recent (2018) in our collection. The importance and function of salt, fat, acid, and heat. An inspiring book.

———

We've culled these books out of a collection of 50 to 60 cookbooks.

- *Mrs. Restino's Country Kitchen* by Susan Restino

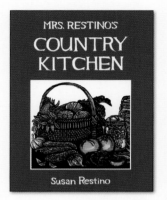

Shelter's one and only cookbook. Suzy and Charlie Restino moved to a farm in Nova Scotia in the early '70s, planted a large garden, raised chickens and goats, and ate mostly what they produced. This is Suzy's story of cooking from the garden.

Alice Waters: "I like the impulse of this book — grow your own and make your own."

Foraging, Fishing

Seaweed

I pick up clean seaweed on the beach or harvest it in the waters of the ocean or bay. I dry it (we have an electric dehydrator with 10 trays, which we use for seaweed, as well as mushrooms; in years past we've used it for drying apples).

Once dry, I grind it in the Blendtec blender *(see p. 32)* and then sprinkle it on many types of food. It's a great source of vitamins, minerals, and protective antioxidants.

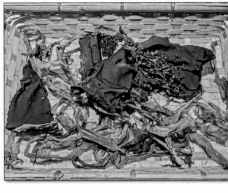

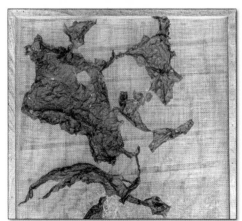

Acorns

Acorns were a primary food for Northern California coastal natives. Those from tan oaks are among the best varieties.

After grinding into flour, it is necessary to remove the bitter tannins; this is a laborious process. The next time I do it, I'm going to try putting the flour in a cheesecloth sack and suspending it under a waterfall in a nearby creek.

We've used it about 50-50 with wheat in pancakes and muffins. It has a nutty flavor.

Watercress

Grows in running water, and is used in salads or on sandwiches.

Miner's Lettuce

Also used in salads.

Cattails

Cattails have so many uses, they are called the "supermarket of nature." I use them in two ways:

- **Shoots** You pull up the stalk, trim off the roots, and the lower part is tender, crunchy, a bit like bamboo shoots, and we use them in salads.

- **Pollen** In early summer, when the heads are covered with bright yellow pollen, you take a paper bag, put it over the head, and shake. It can then be added to pancakes or muffins.

Berries

We have tons of blackberries in the summertime. We freeze some and Lesley makes jam.

Around here we also gather huckleberries and small amounts of thimbleberries. One time I gathered some Manzanita berries on the mountain and made Manzanita cider.

Books on Wild Foods

The Flavors of Home: A Guide to the Wild Edible Plants of the San Francisco Bay Area, by Margit Roos-Collins. Published in 1990, this is a wonderful book on gathering wild foods in the San Francisco Bay Area. I've used it extensively.

Another very good book, useful throughout the United States, is *Nature's Garden: A Guide to Identifying, Harvesting, and Preparing Wild Edible Plants*, by Partners/West Book Distribution.

Mushrooms

I've been hunting for mushrooms for about 10 years. There are four edible types of mushrooms that I'm sure of: chanterelles, porcinis (*Boletus edulis*), blewits (*Clitocybe nuda*), and candy caps.

We have to watch out in our part of the world for the *Amanita phalloides*, or "death caps," among the most poisonous mushrooms in the world, which destroy the liver and kidneys.

I'm lucky to have my friend Tomás (*at right*), a botanist and fungus hunter *extraordinaire*, to consult on all the different species I gather. Lesley cautions me not to eat any mushroom unless I've run it by him. He invariably knows the Latin name and edibility of anything I find.

It's a great pastime in many ways: walking in the woods, getting exercise, the hopefulness of the hunt, the thrill of finding a robust bunch of them.

On this page: Boletus edulis, *(King Bolete), or porcini; prized for its flavor, fresh or dried.*

52

Above and below left: Chanterelles; *colorful, flavorful, sought after*

Laccaria amethystina; *probably best not to eat, because pollutants in the soil, such as arsenic, can accumulate in it.*

Above and below: Lactarius camphoratus, *or candy caps; edible. Delightful: when dried, they give off a strong odor of maple syrup.*

Black chanterelles; *rare in these parts*

Amanita muscaria, *or fly agaric; colorful, abundant, somewhat toxic if not prepared properly, and hallucinogenic.*

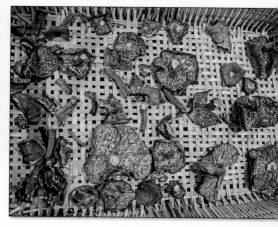

Fishing

I'm the dunce fisherman of my family. My grandfather had a bait and tackle shop in San Francisco in the early 1900s (and made bamboo fishing rods), my dad was a fresh and salt water fisherman, my brother Bob has for years had a Monterey double-ender, my brother Carl fished commercially for a while. And me —I guess I just don't have the patience— if they're not biting, I'm outta there. But, I'm trying to increase my seafood intake.

Striped Bass

I've been fishing for stripers lately (so far with very little luck). What I like is the simplicity. No boat necessary, you cast from shore, and you use a lure rather than bait. You can keep a rod in your car and be ready to fish at any time you see bird action along the coast.

Ocean Fishing

I've got a 12′ aluminum Klamath boat with an old (rebuilt) 15-HP Evinrude 2-stroke outboard motor.

About 20 years ago, I was taking it out into the ocean from here, which is tricky because you have to go through waves, and this boat is smaller than almost all other local ocean-going boats.

One of the first times I took it out, I tried to punch through a wave. Mistake! The boat went about four feet in the air, the propeller revved up, and when it came back down in the water, it stalled. I was in the wave zone, and when I tried pulling on the starter rope, it came off. I grabbed the oars and barely avoided being capsized. Lesson learned.

Also, launching from the beach is a bit tricky due to shifting sands, tides, and swell; it's different every day.

I've caught the occasional salmon and halibut, and rockfish (when there were more of them here). I may get back into it when I finish this book.

Rockfish

While salmon fishing is a bit exotic and difficult, and catching halibut requires skill, fishing for rockfish is perfect for someone with minimal skills. You have three hooks with squid for bait and a weight; you lower the line down until the weight hits the bottom, pull it up a few feet and "jig," pulling the rod up and down.

The Sea Forager

Kirk Lombard is known as the Sea Forager, and he leads tours of various types in the San Francisco area, takes people clamming or herring-catching, and has a seafood subscription service.

Small Fish

He points out that there are numerous small fish in this area — smelt, sand dabs, herring, sardines, grunion, and anchovies — that are overlooked by commercial fishermen (except for herring) and perfect for the get-it-yourselfers.

I went out one night last year with Kirk, fishing with nets for ocean smelt.

These are beautiful little fish. They come in to sandy beaches after dark during the quarter moon to spawn and there we were with our triangular nets (based on a Native American design). We hit it! I ended up with 16 lbs.

A-frame net for night smelt

Only thing is, as I was rinsing them off, a rogue wave knocked me over — soaked to the skin, waders and all. This was like 9:30 PM and it was cold, but I was so stoked, I didn't care. I changed into dry clothes and took off for home with my bounty.

Kirk has written a great book: *The Sea Forager's Guide to the Northern California Coast.* If you live in the San Francisco

*Grunion, a small fish that comes in late at night on high tides to lay its eggs in the sand.
Best cooked at high temperatures. At right, filleting them to pickle.*

Bay Area and are interested in fishing—
or getting fresh fish—his website is
www.seaforager.com.

Monkeyface Eels

Although they are commonly called eels,
they are actually monkeyface prickleback
fish. They live in deep cracks in shoreline
rocks. I use a 20´-long "poke pole" with
a short leader and a piece of squid to
catch them.

*Preparing, below 3 photos: Take a short 1×6 board with three 16-penny nails driven through
it. With a rubber mallet, pound the eel's head so it's held securely by nails. Cut skin along both
sides and top with a very sharp knife. Grasp skin at top with pliers and pull it off, then filet.
We dip in flour and cook in olive oil/butter at high temperature.*

Shellfish

There are four types of shellfish that I get around here:

- **Littleneck clams**, averaging 1½ to 2 inches in diameter, which live a few inches below the surface on rocky, sandy shores. I rake for these with a triangular hoe.

- **Horseneck clams**, which are maybe two feet deep in the mud. Most people dig for them — it's a lot of work. Another method is to use a (homemade) clam gun:

Clam gun made of 3″ PVC pipe, stainless steel threaded rod, by Eloy Garcia (who taught me the technique)

When you see the telltale hole of a horse-neck in the mud, you place the gun on top of the siphon hole and pump out the mud until you can reach down and grab the clam. *(See p. 42 for clam fritters.)*

- **Rock oysters**, which sometimes escape from the commercial oyster beds and can be found clinging to rocks; they can get to be quite large.
- **Mussels**, which are abundant in the ocean and bays, but during the warmer months (generally between May 1 and October 31), they may contain danger-ous levels of biotoxins.

Crabs

Dungeness crabs are among the miracle foods of the San Francisco Bay area. Commercial crab season hereabouts is currently from November 15 through June. Sports fishing season generally opens on November 1. Minimum size is 6½ inches.

These crabs are scavengers of the ocean bottom and have been a sustainable food source for hundreds of years.

For small boats like mine, there are lightweight crab pots such as this one:

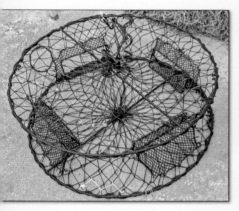

Another method of catching them is to use an ingenious device, the crab snare:

A piece of bait is placed inside the box, which is then cast out into the water with a fishing rod. You let it sit for 10 to 15 minutes, then reel it in. Crabs that have been trying to get the bait are snared with the nylon loops.

Rock crabs The season is open year-round; minimum size is 4 inches. There is not much meat in the body, but the claws are large (called "Popeye arms").

The Production Studio/Office

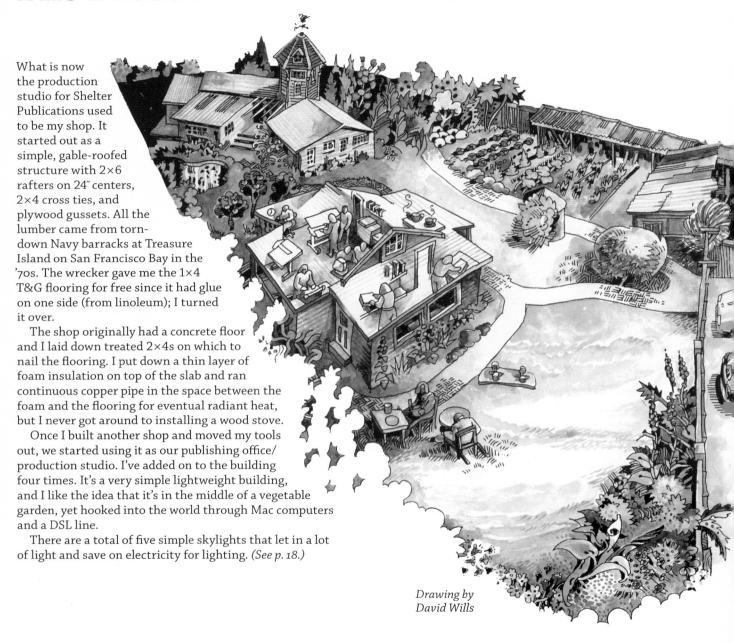

What is now the production studio for Shelter Publications used to be my shop. It started out as a simple, gable-roofed structure with 2×6 rafters on 24″ centers, 2×4 cross ties, and plywood gussets. All the lumber came from torn-down Navy barracks at Treasure Island on San Francisco Bay in the '70s. The wrecker gave me the 1×4 T&G flooring for free since it had glue on one side (from linoleum); I turned it over.

The shop originally had a concrete floor and I laid down treated 2×4s on which to nail the flooring. I put down a thin layer of foam insulation on top of the slab and ran continuous copper pipe in the space between the foam and the flooring for eventual radiant heat, but I never got around to installing a wood stove.

Once I built another shop and moved my tools out, we started using it as our publishing office/ production studio. I've added on to the building four times. It's a very simple lightweight building, and I like the idea that it's in the middle of a vegetable garden, yet hooked into the world through Mac computers and a DSL line.

There are a total of five simple skylights that let in a lot of light and save on electricity for lighting. *(See p. 18.)*

*Drawing by
David Wills*

Computer Workstation

I think it's good to have a stand/sit option. I try to be upright as much as possible, and when standing, use a 24″ by 36″ anti-fatigue kitchen WellnessMat. I also have a high stool for sitting.

My iMac is 47″ high at the base. The keyboard/mouse table is 38″ high. I slide the WellnessMat under the desk when sitting.

shltr.net/hah9

My computer is set up so that I stand (or sit) with my back to the door. One day a friend who understands the art of *feng shui* came by and said that I should put a mirror on the wall to the side and behind my computer so that I could see anyone coming into the room. This completely changed the dynamics of the workspace. It made a huge difference.

Hardware

I have a 27″ iMac and a Dell 24″ monitor; Rick, our director of production, works at home with a Mac Pro tower with two NEC monitors; Mary, our office manager, has a 24″ iMac; and Evan uses a 24″ iMac, and a MacBook Pro laptop with a 24″ Dell monitor. We have three printers: a Hewlett Packard Laserjet Pro 400 for black and white, an inexpensive Brother MFC 9130 CW color printer that I use for layout, and a wonderful Epson Stylus Pro 4900 for high-quality color printing.

In the tiny kitchen we have an iRoast coffee roaster, a Solis coffee grinder, and an old Rancilio Sylvia espresso machine. We buy green Malabar Gold coffee beans via mail order from the Coffee Project.

www.coffeeproject.com

Crafts

Lloyd: Lesley has been making things most of her life. When we first got together, she had a job sewing leather purses, and she was making a lot of her own clothes.

Throughout the years, she has continued making things by hand. She varies between crafts. For many years, she worked on quilts. Every day she knits: hats, scarves; she's even knitted me fingerless gloves for cold mornings at the keyboard. Her passion lately has been spinning and weaving.

On the following pages are some of the things she's made.

Lesley: I have always liked learning how people made things in the past; they did so much more for themselves — not only with food production and preparation, but with making things necessary in their everyday lives.

In sewing, I've made practical things for the house: curtains, blankets, pot holders, tea cozies, dishcloths, bags, pillows, and clothes.

It was a great breakthrough to realize I could sew for fun. Quilts, purses, hats, and fanny packs.

Also, through the years, pine needle baskets, beading, and simple jewelry.

In recent years, I've taken up weaving — spinning, and dying yarn for shawls, scarves, and blankets, as well as for knitting.

There's always something new to learn — making things that are useful, practical, and beautiful.

Quilting

Lesley: Maybe because there was no quilting tradition in my family, I felt free to "play" with color and pattern. I've been influenced by early American quilts — mostly Amish — as well as folk traditions in Europe, and African-American quilts, as shown in the collection of Eli Leon. All of these have shown me the possibilities of play.

I always start with colors, then the pattern. Recently I've been drawn to more abstract patterns, and and a more neutral palette, using recycled clothing and "found" materials (see p. 67 for some of the most recent ones).

After planning and cutting all the pieces, I sew a quilt together on my sewing machine (allowing random color combinations), and then spend a month or two quilting by hand — a little every day.

88˝ by 100˝

56″ by 66″

60″ by 70″

56″ by 70″

50″ by 65″

47″ by 70″

64″ by 67″

58″ by 78″

70″ by 85″

65″ by 75″

68″ by 88″

68″ by 70″

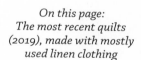
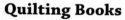

*On this page:
The most recent quilts
(2019), made with mostly
used linen clothing*

Quilting Books

101 Patchwork Patterns, by Ruby McKim.
Literary Licensing, LLC

Plaids and Stripes, by Roberta Horton.
C&T Publishing

Old Swedish Quilts, by Asa Wettre and
Lena Nessle. Interweave Press

*Who'd a Thought It: Improvisation
in African-American Quiltmaking*,
by Eli Leon. San Francisco Craft
and Folk Art Museum

78″ by 80″

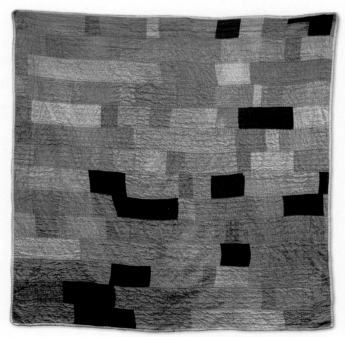

72″ by 74″

Spinning and Weaving

Lesley: I've been spinning and weaving over the last 10 years. There is still much to learn; I consider myself a beginner. I make simple, useful shawls and blankets, mostly with commercial alpaca and merino wool.

Lately, I've been starting from scratch, taking fleece sheared from the sheep, sorting and washing it, carding it (brushing the fibers parallel), and then spinning it on my upright spinning wheel. I dye the resulting yarn with either natural or commercial dyes.

I do most of my weaving these days on a 42″-wide, four-shaft Gilmore jack loom.

There is always something new to discover. It's thrilling to be part of the long tradition of fiber work.

Why Buy When You Can Make!

"Why buy when you can make," is a formula followed by Mark Hanson, a prolific builder (of sailboats, gypsy wagons, tents, birch-bark canoes, camper vans, and many other things) in Minnesota. Mark said this to me when I was photographing his work for *Tiny Homes on the Move* several years ago.

It's a mindset, followed by most of the builders covered in our books, and I feel the same way. I try to make simple things (usually ones that can be made out of wood), that we need in everyday life. Tables, beds, drawers, cabinets, bookshelves, gate handles, etc. Rather than running to IKEA or looking for something on Amazon.

Tables

These four tables are made with used 2″, 3″, 4″ Douglas fir.

Little lightweight table made with 2×4s and inexpensive cedar fence wood from Home Depot, put together with construction screws, took about an hour to build.

Made out of old (split) redwood fence posts. I copied a popular local garden chair. I split out the backrest boards. The next one, I'll split out the seat boards too (here I used dimensional lumber). I sanded edges with belt/disc sander.

Scrap of frayed Oriental rug to recover old bamboo stool. Attached with brass upholstery tacks.

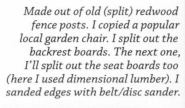

Replacement for broken crock top

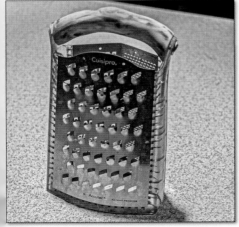

Broken handle replaced with manzanita branch

Two sides of door, built of of rough used 1″ Douglas fir, put together with nails, in the '70s. (Gun-driven construction screws hadn't been invented.)

Left and above: Wine cork boards; corks glued to pieces of plywood

It's fun finding driftwood for handles on the beaches, branches for hangers in the woods.

Paring knife handles. I bought the blades and made wood handles out of found pieces of hardwood, attached with brass rivets.

Rusty Art

Vintage Tonka toys

About 40 years old. Still rolls perfectly.

*Old sauna stove
— relegated to garden
when it developed cracks.*

Small-Scale Farming in the '70s

At the same time that I was building, we had a vegetable garden, and within a few years, we added chickens, goats, and bees. I was hiring out as a carpenter from time to time, and running the publishing company in a minimal way. Lesley was running the garden, and working with me on books and mail-order sales.

In 1975, we had kindred spirits among our neighbors, all of whom built their own homes:

1. Michael and Vickisa had a large garden, a cow, chickens, and bees. I learned how to keep bees from Michael.

2. Bob and Sabina had a big productive garden and an amazing number of animals on a small plot of land — about half an acre. A cow, a few pigs, a few sheep, chickens, geese, and ducks.

3. Jack and Nina had a cow, chickens, a big vegetable garden, and were dedicated to minimal resource consumption.

The four of us couples were in close touch with our homesteading pursuits, learning from one another, having meals and tea and coffee together, comparing notes.

One thing about all this (in retrospect, it was a privilege to have the time to try stuff out) — it was fun! It was good, clean work; preparing soil and nourishing plants was endlessly satisfying; and organic food turned out to be — delicious!

Larger Local Organic and Natural Food Production

People with more land on the outskirts of our town were starting to produce organic produce and range-fed beef and pork:

1. Warren Weber was starting Star Route Farms. (See "Organic Farming Movement" at right.)

2. Dennis and Sandy Dierks were starting Paradise Valley Produce. Both of these farms were early organic farm operations of serious size.

3. Bill Niman and Orville Schell started Niman-Schell Meats, which eventually became Niman Ranch, and is still in operation nationally with humane, non-GMO, (partially) range-fed animals raised by small farmers.

Michael Gaspers and I leased 10 acres of land from the utility district for farming in 1975.

Michael and I also hung out with Arnold Brost, in his 60s, a German who had grown up in Bessarabia (now Moldavia and Ukraine) in a family of farmers who had moved there from Germany. He was Old World. He knew how to grow wheat, keep bees (when he moved back to Germany, before coming to America, he had 49 hives); he knew how to slaughter pigs and smoke hams, how to make cream of tartar from grape skins, make wine, gather wild herbs, how to prune fruit trees.

Michael and I would visit him, and sit around drinking homemade wine in his trailer, learning all kinds of things about growing and processing food. Arnold would come over to my place, light a cigarette, and work with my bees — no protective gear; he and the bees liked each other. He often got the bees to sting him on the arms, saying it helped his arthritis.

Organic Farming Movement

In looking back, what was happening in our small town was part of a state, then national, move towards widespread acceptance of organic foods. For example, in 1974, Warren Weber, with Star Route Farms, was working his farm land with two large draft horses.

On our leased land, Michael and I decided to plant five acres of permanent pasture, two acres of oats and vetch for hay, and several acres in experimental strips of wheat, rye, triticale, and garlic. I made a deal with Warren: If he would use his seed drill* for planting our crops, I'd give him an equal amount of tractor time.

Warren came up with his horses and drill, and we seeded our acreage. The next morning I took the tractor down and he had me plow one of his fields. He watched as I pulled the lever of the 3-point hitch and the disc harrow bit into the soil, and then I quickly disced the field.

He was obviously impressed by the speed of the operation, as he'd been struggling for several years to do everything with horses. Within a month, the horses were gone and he had a tractor.

Soon, Warren was supplying Alice Waters' new restaurant Chez Panisse with organic baby lettuces, and he went on to become one of the founders of the California Certified Organic Farmers (CCOF) group, which, it could be argued, paved the way for national acceptance of organic produce.

Local Farmers' Market

We started having our own small farmers' market in town. (More accurately, it was

---

A device (in this case, horse-drawn) that sows seeds under the surface of the soil, and covers them up.

gardeners' market.) Maybe a dozen people would sell vegetables. Chuck, a local fishermen, sold fresh fish filets. I would go to Sebastopol and load apples from abandoned orchards in my pickup truck, make apple juice with a wine press, and sell it for $2 a half gallon. We sold eggs for $1 a dozen and honey for $1 a pound. Lesley sold English muffins for 15 cents apiece. Pearl sold chocolate-coated cookies. It was also a chance for all of us to get together and compare notes.

Cooperative Food Buying

We formed a food club, maybe 20 families, and we bought bulk food wholesale. We ordered grains, flour, beans, apple juice, rice crackers, etc., and had a load delivered by truck about once a month. Each month one of us would go into San Francisco to pick up bulk orders of cheese and vegetables. People would show up at someone's designated house and pick up their goods. We probably saved 40 percent or so buying this way.

The Times Were Right for Trying Stuff Out

It was easy to experiment back then. Living was cheap. We built our homes on the pay-as-you-go basis. We had no rent or mortgage payments. There was maybe a 15-year period in America when livin' was easy. You could survive on very little, and this gave us time to try stuff out.

A Small-Scale Piece of Land

Chickens We've had chickens for over 35 years. For the eggs, meat, and simplicity, they're well worth the effort. Once you have home-grown eggs, you'll never want store-bought eggs. *(See pp. 116–121.)*

Bees I tended bees for maybe 10 years; they are fascinating creatures, a species that is 85 million years old. But eventually, it was too much work. We couldn't make money selling honey, and we

didn't consume that much, so I got rid of the bees.

By the way, by following suggestions of Santa Cruz beekeepers Ormond and Harry Aebi in their book *The Art & Adventure of Beekeeping,* which involved how you stacked supers during the summer months, I got 300 pounds of honey from one hive during one year. The hive was stacked about 11′ tall.

Goats We had them for 8 to 10 years, and they were the most difficult of our food-producing animals. Fresh goats' milk is wonderful, but tending dairy animals turned out to be an enormous responsibility. They have to be milked twice a day, rain or shine. They don't take holidays. The hygienic requirements for dairy animals are serious; you've got to keep things scrupulously clean. I concluded that half an acre is not a large enough piece of land for dairy animals, Eventually we got rid of the goats. It was a great relief, a lot less daily work.

We Couldn't Make It as Small-Scale Farmers

By 1973, I had published *Domebook One, Domebook 2,* and *Shelter.* I was by then more interested in building, farming, and gardening than publishing, and thought I was through producing books. I wanted to see if we could make a living producing organic food.

It soon became apparent that it wouldn't work. One dollar for a quart of organic goats' milk, $1 for a dozen free-range eggs, $1 for a pound of honey, $2 for a half gallon of fresh apple juice, $1 for a loaf of stone-ground whole wheat bread—it just wasn't enough.

In those days, there wasn't much demand for organic food, and people wouldn't pay extra for it. We couldn't make a living on this basis. If we'd had enough land to do some real-scale farming, we might have made a go of it.

Yet I was fascinated with farming, gardening, building, and doing all the things that homesteaders had done in the 1800s. I was excited to be growing wheat (experimentally), tending bees and chickens, and enriching and improving the soil. I remember thinking, here I am, a Stanford graduate, a dropped-out insurance executive, foregoing a lucrative career, and thrilled to be driving a tractor, building my own house, transforming chicken shit and compost scraps into rich, black soil, figuring out how much of our own food and shelter we could provide for our family.

Pamphlets on Local Food Production

In 1975 to '76, a group of us produced three small publications on farming and food production in our area.

We interviewed old-time locals, did surveys of all the current food production in our town and environs, covered farming history, published greenhouse plans, described various ways of using natural materials in building homes, and had photos and drawings of barns and farm buildings. Our purpose was to maximize our own local food production.

Gardening for Two People

Lesley is the gardener, the family farmer, as well as the landscape designer. My main contribution is tending the compost pile. I don't do 5 percent of the gardening these days.

Lesley: I like the fresh air and exercise, listening to the birds, watching butterflies, attracting wildlife, seeing things improve over time, producing delicious food and beautiful flowers, and the peace and tranquility of spending time in the garden.

We don't grow all our own vegetables, but even two to three kale plants will provide frequent greens for a large part of the year. The challenge in a small garden for just a couple of people is to grow small amounts — and of course it's great to share excess with friends.

We have a simple plan to take advantage of our coastal California weather. Hot weather crops are a bit of a struggle here, but we can grow greens year round.

The **basic vegetable garden** consists of: lettuce, chard, spinach, broccoli, and kale; garlic, leeks, and onions; beets, chives, parsley; potatoes, zucchini, peas, pea pods, and green beans. Asparagus and artichokes. Various herbs, including basil, dill, cilantro.

We grow corn every year or two. Parsley, rhubarb, Brussels sprouts, fava beans (for both the beans and to dig in for green manure).

This last year Lesley had success with small cantaloupes in the greenhouse. Each year she also grows tomatoes, cucumbers, and various peppers in one of the greenhouses.

Berries

Raspberries (a fairly large, old stand), lots of wild blackberries, a few bushes of blueberries and red currants, and periodically some strawberries.

Fruit Trees

We have five apple trees, a green gauge plum, a few lemon trees, a fig tree (which struggles to ripen its figs before winter sets in), a mulberry tree, which hasn't yet produced satisfactorily. We also belatedly planted three olive trees.

In retrospect, I'd plant more olive trees, a couple of mulberry trees (trees that have berries!), and timber bamboo.

The Soil

Our soil is black and rich, but it's taken decades to get it loose enough. It started out very heavy in clay and has taken a long time and much addition of organic matter to get it loose and friable. Every scrap of leftover food from 40+ years has been composted and is in the soil. Over the years, we've built it up way above its natural level.

We've kept working on our home and garden to this day. It's a never-ending process.

Hopefully, at least a few of the things we've done over the years will resonate with you and be useful.

The Miracle of Seeds

It never fails to amaze me that a seed is like an instruction manual, or a recipe — organizing the soil, sun, moisture and air to produce exactly what's listed on the seed packet. A miracle!

Alan Chadwick's Gardening Methods

In the mid-'70s, we discovered Alan Chadwick and his biodynamic French intensive system of gardening. Up to then I'd used a rototiller in digging beds.

Allen's system involved double digging with hand tools, producing *raised beds,* and the results were spectacular. I got rid of the Rototiller and we haven't tilled the soil since. (If you are going to use a tiller, the Troy Bilt is a dependable — and made-in-USA — machine.)

Alan Chadwick created "The Farm" at UC Santa Cruz, California, established the gardens at Green Gulch Zen Center in Marin County, California, and with much help, created magnificent gardens in Round Valley (near Covelo), California.

In about 1975, I went to a seminar/lunch in Covelo and heard Alan talk.

He said that if a plant had aphids or some other disease, it meant that the

plant was weak, and nature was trying to compost it.

If you keep your plants strong and give them the air, water, sunshine, and nutrients that they need, they will be healthy and resist disease.

He also explained that with the raised beds, the plants — roots and vegetation — had more access to air, water, sunshine, and planetary vibrations as well as influence from the moon in their growth cycle. Wow!

You can read about Alan's techniques at ***www.alan-chadwick.org***.

The "Gardener of Souls"

For Alan, "beauty was an uplifting spiritual force that carried within it the ability to heal human souls that had become estranged from nature."

–Adapted from an article by Greg Haynes on the Chadwick website

Ornamentals

Lesley: On our small plot of land, along with the vegetables, greenhouses, and fruit trees, there is plenty of room for ornamentals. Hedges provide privacy, wind protection and a haven for birds. Various plants, including flowers, smell good and encourage bees and butterflies, birds and beneficial insects. Spending time in the garden is always uplifting, showing that "life" can always be protected and improved with care.

Raised Beds

We live in gopher land, and after losing innumerable plants to these subterranean pests for years, we started building raised beds with ¼″ galvanized mesh along the bottom. We have a total of seven raised beds these days, and grow almost all of our vegetables in them.

Concrete block beds Lesley built the first one of these. Very simple: you lay the ¼″ mesh on the ground, stack two layers of concrete blocks (no mortar needed), and fill in with soil.

Be sure to have the mesh extend several inches on the outside of the low block walls.

You can plant things like parsley or strawberries in the block cavities.

Wooden beds I also built two beds using 2×12 rough redwood planks, with two galvanized 1½×6 angle brackets bolted on at each corner. For anyone living in Marin County, Goodman's Building Supply offers a 15 percent discount on all purchases made on Sundays — this helps with the high cost of redwood these days.

Five photos: Construction of concrete block beds

Three photos, below and opposite page: Wooden beds

Raised bed built of shakes by Bruno Atkey on Vancouver Island

The photo below shows a lightweight bird cover (when we're growing strawberries in the beds) made out of cedar fence boards ripped to 3″, with plastic garden netting.

The Well

In 1980 we decided to dig a shallow well for watering the garden. The father of one of our friends, Bob Scott, was visiting one day and said that he knew something about dowsing. He broke off a piece of coyote bush so that it was like a large wishbone. He held it in both hands and walked around the garden. At a certain point, the tip bent down forcibly. "There's water here," he said.

I had seen a method of dowsing described in the book *Secret Discoveries Behind the Iron Curtain,* using a reconfigured coat hanger, and I got the same results at the same spot; the wire dipped dramatically.

Bill Tacherra dug the well for us with his backhoe. It was about 15 feet deep by 10 feet in diameter. Bill took a 15´-long piece of 8˝-diameter ABS pipe, cut saw kerfs in it (for water infiltration), placed it upright in the middle of the hole, filled the hole in with gravel, then backfilled in the soil. I installed a Dayton ½-HP shallow-well jet pump and a 1¼´ piece of 1¼´ PVC pipe down the middle of the 8˝ pipe, and an 80-gallon pressure tank.

Well house

It's worked well for some 35 years. In years of low rainfall, it dries up for maybe two months in October and November, but recently it's worked throughout the year.

About three years ago I installed a new pump and a new pressure tank.

Greywater

The easiest way to utilize greywater is to divert washing machine water into a barrel, which has a hose you can move around in the garden. With other sources of greywater — bathroom sink, bath/shower — diverter valves can be installed. For details on many approaches to utilizing greywater, go to Art Ludwig's ***www.oasisdesign.net***.

Rainwater Catchment

We started adding rainwater-catching containers as time went by. An inch of rain, when collected off a broad expanse of roof, can provide many gallons of water.

Compost Piles

I built three bins, 5′ wide, 5′ deep, and 5′ high. At the back is corrugated metal roofing. The posts are 8×8 redwood with grooves dadoed out in the front and sides — so I can slide 1′ boards in and adjust the height in the front and two sides according to how much compost is in each bin.

In the bin shown at the left in this photo, I put kitchen scraps, grass cuttings, oak leaves, clam shells, chicken shit, etc. Every few years, I'll buy some worms and introduce them to the pile. I'll mix the ingredients up with a pitchfork. I have a frame with chicken wire on it to keep out raccoons and skunks. I keep a tarp on top to retain moisture.

When the pile gets high enough, it gets turned into the adjacent bin *(bottom photo)* — by which time it's pretty well composted, and I start over again with the initial pile. Lesley then uses the finished compost when planting vegetables.

It's a continual wonder to see smelly food scraps, green grass, and oak leaves turned into black, sweet-smelling, rich soil by the worms and soil microorganisms.

Note: If you live in an urban or suburban area, but don't want to go to all this trouble, I recommend a composting tumbler; these are closed, so animals (including rats) can't get in, and the tumbling action speeds up the composting process. I've never used one so I don't know which ones to recommend, but I would avoid the cheap ones; they look pretty flimsy.

I would think you'd need two of them so that one could be used for fresh scraps, and the other for letting the material sit (with periodic tumbling) until composted.

You can also get worm bins (vermicomposters) that can be used inside the house.

I have used corrugated metal roofing in conjunction with fences to make spaces for tools, firewood, compost, and lumber. I got a lot of this heavy-duty steel roofing, used, in the '70s, for about $2 per sheet. It was from docks in the San Francisco waterfront that were being torn down.

The fence is already there, so there's a back wall to start with. The roofing panels are strong enough to span from the fence to a plate on poles eight feet away, with no rafters necessary.

Initial composting bin. I turn the contents as I add new food and garden scraps.

Secondary bin, where it's turned after the first bin gets high enough, and the material is pretty well composted.

Pond

I built this maybe 25 years go. Joslin Brothers pumped the concrete (way better than trying to do it with the truck chute and wheelbarrows). Art Moritz set the stones around the edge (and taught me how to do it).

We've had various fish in it, including some decent-sized Koi over the years. We also had a pump that circulated the water. One year a wily raccoon pulled the pump outflow hose so the pond drained and he got the fish. (A way to avoid raccoon fish-pilferage is to put a few 2′- to 3′-long, 1′-diameter sections of ceramic pipe in the bottom of the pond; the fish will get inside when those *bandido* paws start coming down into the water.)

One of the best things about the pond is the rare visit of a blue heron or an egret. We have a big window in the house right in front of the pond, so we can get pretty close to these elegant birds without them being aware of us. *(See pp. 124-125.)*

They'll stand there on one leg, motionless and then — wham! — they'll spear a fish.

We stopped using a pump years ago; the pond does fine on its own. The water lilies thrive, with no care. Periodically, Lesley skims the algae off the surface, puts it in 5-gallon buckets, and I incorporate it into the compost pile.

Pond in spring with blossoms from ornamental cherry tree

Pond in summer when water lilies thrive

Pond in fall

Living Roof

This is the roof of our chicken coop, built several years ago by Billy, Marco, and me. It's coming full circle, in a way, for me, since my first-ever building project, in 1961, was a studio with living roof. In those days we called them sod roofs. *(See p. 156.)*

Following are a few facts about construction of this roof. (I'm not going to go into detail here, since a living roof is a complex project. If you're considering doing one, I suggest a lot of research.)

In this case, we used a pond liner for the waterproofing, then lava rock and gravel underneath for drainage, then topsoil and rice hulls.

Another waterproofing system, used by many builders in the Pacific Northwest, is to use the Torch Down process, which consists of rolls of a modified bitumen material, sealed at the edges with a blowtorch.

There are a lot of steps here, including finding shallow-soil plants that won't bottom out, and making sure rain water moves through the soil and gravel to drain properly.

Living roofs look great, and they provide great insulation, but there's a cost in time, materials, and money. First, the roof framing must be substantially stronger to support the weight of the wet soil. Secondly, it's essential that the waterproofing system works. If it doesn't, you're going to be removing tons of soil to locate the leak.

It was a lot of work, but it's sure easy on the eyes (say, compared to an expanse of asphalt shingles). We look out on this from the kitchen sink and the dining room table.

Flowers

On the following pages are photos of flowers that I've taken over the years. I'll be walking along a path in the garden, and something will catch my eye. Every year, every season, every day is different, and the delight is never-ending.

Sunflower

Hollyhock, Alcea rosea

Alstromeria, *or lily of the Incas*   *Photo: Lesley Creed*

Lily

Sometimes, when I see something stunning in the natural world, I think of Ricky, the kid with the video camera in the film *American Beauty,* who said:

"There's so much beauty in the world. Sometimes I feel like I'm seeing it all at once, and it's too much; my heart fills up like a balloon that's about to burst . . . and then I remember to relax, and stop trying to hold on to it, and then it flows through me like rain and I can't feel anything but gratitude."

Puya alpestris, *or Sapphire Tower*

Oriental or bread seed poppies, Papaver somniferum
are cultivated for their beauty, for seeds (as in
poppyseed bagels), and in Afghanistan for their
narcotic alkaloids, which are the active compounds of
opium. They are beautiful and intricate in structure.
Honeybees love the pollen.

Top two photos: Papaver hybridium, *or orange chiffon poppies*

This page: Papaver rhoeas, *or corn poppies*

Water lily

Dahlia

Sparaxis, *or Harlequin Flower*

Rose

Artichoke

Antirrhinum

Yarrow

Dahlia

Bidens ferulifolia

California poppy

Delphinium

California poppies

101

Geometry from the Garden

Cylindrical symmetry

Pentagonal symmetry in pomegranate

Four-fold symmetry in this row

> "Human subtlety …
> will never devise an
> invention more beautiful,
> more simple, or more
> direct than does nature,
> because in her inventions
> nothing is lacking, and
> nothing is superfluous."
> –Leonardo da Vinci
> *The Notebooks* (1508–1518)

Romanesco broccoli, with logarithmic spirals (the same as in sunflowers)

15-fold symmetry in oriental poppy

A sort of bilateral symmetry

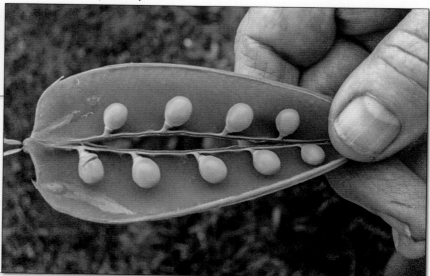

Greenhouses

Main Greenhouse

The rear wall is built of adobe bricks that I made with a Cinva Ram, a "third world" device for making compressed earth blocks. I made the bricks in 1980 with earth dug out for the well. *(See p. 84.)*

They consist of 12 parts soil and one part cement. The mixture is loaded into a mold, which is then compressed, and the result is a stabilized adobe brick. (By the time you've made the bricks, carted them to the building site, and laid the wall, it's a lot of work!) The mass of adobe holds the heat generated each day.

I salvaged the windows in the front from a remodeling project at my brother's house. The greenhouse as it now stands was completely remodeled by our friend Tom about 10 years ago

The first roof I installed consisted of corrugated vinyl panels from Home Depot. This turned out to be a terrible material and was discolored after only a few years.

Next I installed corrugated fiberglass panels; they lasted for maybe 10 years until they were discolored from the sun and algae.

Finally, I used what I should have used in the first place:* double-wall polycarbonate panels. Expensive, but the light coming through this material is beneficial for plants, the double wall provides a measure of insulation, and they have a 10-year guarantee. I got the panels and the connectors (via UPS) from Farmtek, a large farm equipment company in Dyersville, Iowa (**www.farmtek.com**). You can also get these panels from Tap Plastics. I highly recommend this material for greenhouses or skylights.

Simple cold frame built by David Shipway on Cortes Island, BC, Canada

---

Sign in the San Marin Lumber yard office: "If you didn't have time to do it right in the first place, how come you have time to do it over?" Story of my life.

*Inside hoop greenhouse
(showing raised bed)*

Hoop Greenhouse

We got the parts for this greenhouse from Farmtek as well. The structural components are very minimal: ¾″ steel tubing on 4′ centers. The cover is woven rip-stop polyethylene with a 7- to 10-year lifespan. It was a bit tricky getting the cover tight.*

After using it for one year, Lesley decided she wanted it to be higher, so we built low walls, two concrete blocks high, and set the greenhouse on top of that.

We had a lot of help from Billy, Marco, and Evan on this one.

There are raised beds inside, with ¼″ wire mesh along the bottom for gophers. *(See photo at right.)* This makes warm-weather crops like tomatoes, cucumbers, and peppers possible in our cool coastal climate.

Billy built doors at either end for entry and air circulation.

*Our neighbor Todd opted to build, rather than buy a hoop greenhouse; he bent ¾″ plastic pipe, cut short sections of larger pipe to secure the plastic, and used polyethylene. It took time, but cost him very little.

Various orchids

Inside the Greenhouse

Donkey tail sedum

Tillandsias, *members of the* Bromeliad *family, that can grow without soil. Here they are growing in hollowed-out branches of* cholla *cactus, which I brought back from Baja.*

All four photos are Hippeastrum amaryllis.

Inside the Greenhouse

Gloriosa Rothschildiana *(climbing lily)*

Crocus sativas

Cattleya *orchid*

Phalaenopsis *(moth orchid)*

109

Garden Tools

McKissick Mighty Mac Chipper/Shredder

I bought a Mighty Mac shredder/chipper about 25 years ago, and have used it — heavily at times — all these years and, with a few engine repairs and turning the shredder blades around once (they are two-sided), it's worked. This is a "hammer mill" chipper with free-swinging hammer blades for the top-feed hopper, as well as a chipper, a side feed where you put in larger branches (it will grind up a 2×4) at a 90-degree angle to the balanced flywheel blade that runs on the same axle as the shredder blades. This unit has changeable screens so you can adjust from fine to coarse output.

It not only gets rid of trimmed branches, but the chipped-up material is a good green component to add to the compost pile.

Be aware: These are dangerous tools. If you get careless and push down on brush in the hopper and get a sleeve caught in the blades, you'll end up with a mangled (or no) hand.

When I bought the shredder, a guy in the shop showed me how to make a simple pusher out of 2×4s *(at right)*.

I also use a Collins machete for chopping up branches for easy feeding and of course goggles (chips fly), earphones, and gloves.

Mine has a 7 HP Briggs and Stratton motor. The current model has a 10 HP. I wouldn't bother with the electric starter; the rope pull works fine.

Very important tool:

2×4 pusher for pushing stuck vegetation into the blades. The width of the cross piece is a little wider than the lower part of the angled hopper.

Also, Collins machete for chopping vegetation

Two other very important tools:

Ear guards. Ear damage is slow and cumulative. I wear earphones religiously for operating any power tools. And protect your eyes with goggles; chips fly.

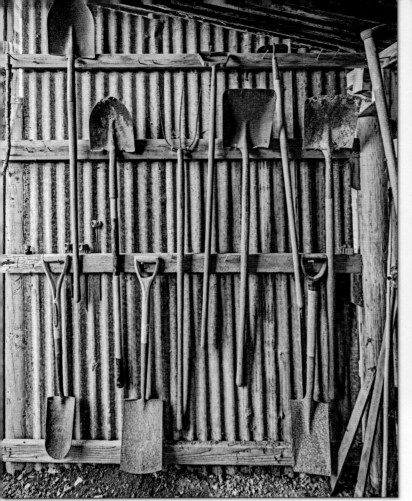

Favorite Gardening Books

- *How to Grow Fruits and Vegetables* by The Royal Horticultural Society
- *The Encyclopedia of Organic Gardening* and *How to Grow Fruits and Vegetables by The Organic Method,* both by J. I. Rodale
- *Better Vegetable Gardens the Chinese Way: Peter Chan's Raised-Bed System* by Peter Chan (1985-04-03)
- *Golden Gate Gardening* by Pam Peirce

Atlas Nitrile Tough garden gloves. They are breathable, tough, tactile (you can pick up seedlings). **shltr.net/hah10**

113

Ameraucana bantam rooster

Chickens

We've been getting baby chicks in the U.S. Mail from Murray McMurray Hatchery in Iowa for 30+ years.

We'll get a call from the postmistress, sometimes a bit flustered, that there's a box there that's peeping. We'll go get them and set them up with a light and feed and water for four weeks, and lo and behold, in five months, we'll have laying hens.

People tend to get a little nutty about chickens. Once you've observed their savvy, and benefitted from their production, you tend not only to respect, but to cherish them. So these pages are for chicken lovers.

(It's the same with bees, or goats, or pigs. Once you raise these animals, you grow to appreciate their skills, and their bounty, especially when raised on a small scale.)

Why get them by mail and not from your local feed store? McMurray has been in business for 90 years and their birds are of excellent stock. Right now, our flock consists mainly of Rhode Island Reds and Auracanas (green eggs) for steady egg production, as well as a few Partridge Rocks and Black Menorcas.

Over the years, we've had maybe 20 different breeds. For five years, we had all bantams, including a number of Golden and Silver Sebrights, beautiful little birds with distinctive feather patterns. *(See p. 119.)*

I suggest getting McMurray's hard copy catalog if you want to start a flock. It's fun just to look through it.

McMurray Hatchery Catalog

www.mcmurrayhatchery.com

(See p. 119.)

A few tips:

1. A dozen hens will give you plenty of eggs for you and neighbors.
2. If you want fertile eggs, plan on ending up with one rooster for every dozen hens.
3. In more urban areas, get 4-5 hens, no rooster.
4. Please don't give your chickens names. Just don't.

We feed all scraps of food to the chickens (other than things like avocado pits or coffee grounds). For example, last night I discovered some mozzarella cheese in the fridge that had turned moldy. The chickens ate it, and it will get processed into eggs, rather than going to the composting bin.

Once you have your own fresh eggs, you'll never want store eggs again.

Once in a while, there will be a chicken-with-personality. This little bantam Rhode Island Red was the first at the door to the yard when we approached, and a wily escape artist. She was perky and curious about everything. She'd cock her head and look up at you. She enjoyed her life.

Chickens not only provide eggs and meat, but also manure for the compost pile—and constant amusement.

Here are some things I find fascinating about chickens; these things are in their DNA:

1. They go inside to roost before sunset, and lay eggs in nests. You don't have to train them; it's in their DNA.
2. They take dust baths to eliminate insects and keep their feathers clean.
3. They remove breast feathers for extra warmth for incubating eggs when setting.
4. They lay eggs for about a month, then set on them, turning them each day and—miracle!—they all hatch at the same time.

Ameraucana hen with two chicks (another two are underneath her).

Ameraucana bantam rooster

Raising Baby Chicks

Whether you get day-old chicks by mail, or buy older chicks at your local feed dealers, read the McMurray Hatchery's Chick Care Tips at *shltr.net/chicks*.

Once you've got a flock (and if you have a rooster), you can let setters raise chicks. We try to avoid cross-breeding, letting setters have only eggs where both hen and rooster are the same breed.

Automatic waterer for chicken yard. Highly recommended.

Lesley made a bunch of tote bags out of feed sack

Sebright Bantams

I fell in love with these beautiful little chickens at the Mendocino County Fair one summer, where I saw a small flock belonging to a 12-year-old 4H girl. Silver Sebrights and Golden Sebrights. They are all bantams; there are no full-size birds. They have striking feathers that are laced around the edges with black.

Looking into it, I discovered that they were bred by Sir John Saunders Sebright in the early 1800s in Hertfordshire, England. Sebright was a colleague of Charles Darwin. In *On the Origin of Species,* first published in 1859, Darwin cited Sir John's experiments in breeding pigeons: "That most skillful breeder, Sir John Sebright, used to say, with respect to pigeons, that he would produce any given feather in three years, but it would take him six years to obtain head and beak."

Sebrights don't lay many eggs, yet we had flocks of them for years — purely for their beauty.

Americauna (Auracana)

Barred Rock

Black Minorca

Australorp

Silver Sebright Bantam

Golden Sebright Bantam

Partridge Cochin Bantam

Black-Tailed White Bantam

Buff Cochin

Ancona

Buttercup

Partridge Rock Bantam

Chickens We Have Known

Info for chicken fanatics only:

Over the past 40+ years, we've had over 20 different breeds, all from the McMurray Hatchery, including Rhode Island Reds, Auracanas, Ameraucanas, Speckled Sussex, Black Australorps, Silver Polish, Buttercups, Partridge Rocks, Black Minorcas, Silver Sebrights, Golden Sebrights, Golden Campines, Lakenvelders, Welsummers, Cuckoo Marans, Buff Cochins, and Golden Pencil Hamburgs.

These are from the McMurray catalog.

White-Crested Black Polish

Silver-Spangled Hamburg

Speckled Sussex

Rhode Island Red

Cuckoo Maran

Welsummer

Birds in Our Lives

Birds are a big part of our lives. We're visited by sparrows, finches, Oregon juncos, rufous-sided towhees, scrub jays, band-tailed pigeons, mourning doves, red-winged blackbirds, red-shouldered hawks, downy woodpeckers, egrets, great blue herons, mockingbirds (once in a while), owls, crows (rude!), ruby-crowned kinglets (friendly), quail (tons of them), and a lot more.

These days, he perches on the door, waiting for me to walk outside with a peanut (upper right).

He got trapped in the studio one day. I captured him and took him outside, but he was so mad at me (look how pissed off he is here) that it was weeks before he'd take a peanut out of my hand again.

Scrub Jays

I have a pal, a scrub jay, that I've been hand-feeding peanuts to for a couple of years. I've trained him to fly to the peanut in my outstretched palm, and snatch it off in flight. He then buries it. I have no idea how he finds the buried peanuts, other that he's a member of the *corvid* family, which includes crows and ravens, some of the smartest animals on the planet.

He was pesky when he was young *(see below left).* He'd come to the (open) office door and squawk in that harsh bluejay manner (which someone compared to the sound of a rusty gate). At times he'd come into the office and perch on the rafter cross ties.

We have a routine: I'll stand in a certain part of the yard, palm extended, with a peanut. He'll hop around in the closest tree, then swoop towards me. If everything isn't right, he'll veer away, then repeat the process. When he decides to get the peanut, he'll skip onto my hand, grab the peanut, and bounce away. I'll feel the wind from his wings. It's always a delight.

This little sparrow ran into a window and was dazed. He recovered and took off.

We see all types of birds bathing here from our dining room table.

California Quail

Quail are like part of our family. They are ground birds, in the chicken (*Phasianidae*) family, scurrying around the garden in big family flocks. In the spring, when the babies are hatched, cats will cut down the number of each hatch. In the winter, they form large flocks.

The male, with the top feather, stands at the highest point as a sentry. If he spots any danger, he'll call out in warning.

The irony of it all: The owl is, of course, intended to scare birds away from the garden.

Great Blue Herons

"Largest of the North American herons with long legs, a sinuous neck, and thick, dagger-like bill. Head, chest, and wing plumes give a shaggy appearance. In flight, the Great Blue Heron curls its neck into a tight 'S' shape; its wings are broad and rounded and its legs trail well beyond the tail."

www.allaboutbirds.org

The occasional visits by egrets *(at left)* and blue herons are a thrill. They're elegant. They come to get the fish in our pond. Blue herons are easily spooked; the slightest motion anywhere and they're gone. They'll perch on top of the tower, some 30 feet off the ground, and if everything looks copacetic, they'll swoop down to the pond and start fishing.

Down the road a piece: turkey vultures drying wings after a storm

Red-winged blackbird. In the spring, they line up on telephone wires and sing in chorus.

Rufous-sided towhee

A Hutton's vereo, a somehow friendly little bird with big eyes. I got within a few feet of it one day, and it was unconcerned.

Mourning dove

Several times a year, a hummingbird will get trapped in the studio. I'll catch it and hold it gently in my hands for a few minutes; I can feel the tiny heart beating. Then open my hands. It'll sit there a minute and then helicopter skyward.

Band-Tailed Pigeons

They travel in big flocks and come here in warmer months. They'll spend a lot of time scouting out any place they're going to land. They are strong-winged aerial acrobats. They're easily alarmed and at the slightest movement or sound, they'll take off, flying straight up like helicopters, with a heavy sound of flapping wings. Not to be confused with city pigeons, or feral pigeons (sometimes called "flying rats").

Red-Shouldered Hawks

We have aviary wire completely covering the chicken yard because of these steely-eyed marauders. As they circle in the air, they make a series of loud "kee-ah" cries, with the second syllable descending in pitch — supposedly to mark their territory. Sometimes they'll come sit on the wire top of the yard (*above*), and the chickens will run inside the coop.

Flight Dreams

I just watched a crow alight in a tree outside the studio. It reminded me of a period about 15 years ago when I dreamed of flying. It was pretty realistic. I wasn't just suddenly in the air; I had to run, flap my arms, and slowly take off. The dreams lasted a couple of weeks. The sensation is still with me; it was thrilling. Once in a while, I'll watch birds, and marvel at their ability. I'm envious.

Animal Visitors

The appropriately named "Sly," our next-door neighbor's cat

Billy's dog, Sophie, wistfully looking for someone (anyone) to throw a stick for her to chase

Native California snail shell, not to be confused with brown garden snails, which were brought from Europe in the 1800s and are now garden pests. Looks to me like a logarithmic spiral.

Garter snake in the pond. Notice how its colors blend in.

Roadkill weasel, a beautiful little animal

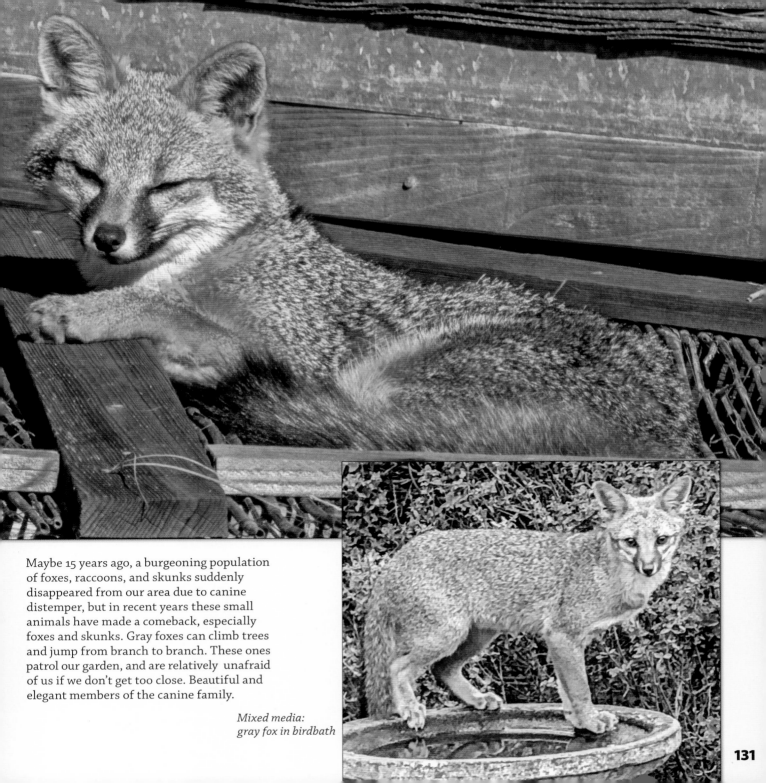

Maybe 15 years ago, a burgeoning population of foxes, raccoons, and skunks suddenly disappeared from our area due to canine distemper, but in recent years these small animals have made a comeback, especially foxes and skunks. Gray foxes can climb trees and jump from branch to branch. These ones patrol our garden, and are relatively unafraid of us if we don't get too close. Beautiful and elegant members of the canine family.

Mixed media: gray fox in birdbath

Butterflies, Caterpillars, Bees, and Other Insects in the Garden

Here are photos of bees, caterpillars, butterflies, spiders, and a few other garden insects. An insect is defined as "having six jointed legs, three body parts — head, thorax (chest), abdomen (tail end), a pair of antennae, compound eyes, and an exoskeleton."

I wondered if butterflies are considered insects, and found this:

"The larval stage of 'Lepidoptera' order of insects (which includes butterflies and moths in general) is called caterpillar. So, basically, we cannot categorize caterpillars as insects as they are one of the life stages of the insect itself. No, caterpillars are very small dragons with tiny legs."

www.quora.com

Monarch butterflies hibernate over winter — usually south of us. In coastal California, our native milkweed plants start growing in late spring; we see butterflies appear in late summer and fall, stopping to lay eggs and continue the cycle before heading south for the winter.

The Four-Stage Life Cycle of a Monarch Butterfly:

1. Egg
2. *Larva* (caterpillar)
3. *Pupa* (chrysalis)
4. Adult butterfly

"It takes about four days for the eggs to hatch into baby caterpillars — also called the larvae — which don't do much more than eat the milkweed in order to grow.

"After about two weeks, the caterpillar will be fully grown and find a place to start the process of metamorphosis. It will attach itself to a stem or a leaf using silk and transform into a chrysalis. Although, from the outside, the 10 days of the chrysalis phase seems to be a time when nothing is happening, it is really a time of rapid change.

"Within the chrysalis, the old body parts of the caterpillar are undergoing a remarkable transformation, called metamorphosis, to become the beautiful parts that make up the butterfly that will emerge.

"The monarch butterfly will emerge from the pupa and fly away, feeding on flowers and just enjoying the short life it has left, which is only about two to six weeks. This first generation monarch butterfly will then die after laying eggs for generation number two."

www.monarch-butterfly.com

L-R: The caterpillar, the chrysalis, and the monarch butterfly. Lesley grows California native milkweed plants to attract the monarchs. When a caterpillar materializes, she watches daily to follow the awesome transformation.

Above: *Anise swallowtail butterfly, a rare visitor. They reproduce on fennel plants.*

Left: *Anise swallowtail caterpillar*

"If you build a garden, they will come — the birds, the bees, and the butterflies"

–*Wings in the Light*
David Lee Myers

Common Calosoma beetles are quick and agile and exude a foul odor if agitated. Skunks of the insect world.

"Small dragon with tiny legs"
Spotted tussock moth caterpillar

"Ladybug, ladybug"

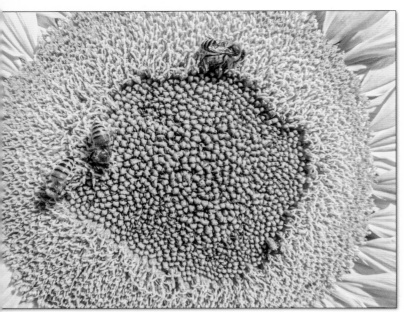

Honeybees working sunflowers

West Coast Lady butterfly, fairly common here

Bee on dahlia

Dew-enhanced spider webs

Pests

This is taken from an article I wrote several years ago for The Mother Earth News. *It seems especially relevant today as I put these pages together, since last night we lost our rooster (defending his flock) and one of our favorites, a Black Minorca to a nighttime raid, due to a rotted-out fence board. I'm setting a trap tonight.*

Fencing, netting, chicken wire, traps, potions, and tools are part and parcel of living at the edge of wilderness. We have to deter pests that want to eat our vegetables, kill our chickens, nest in the woodpile, burrow into our rafters, raid the pantry, and steal whatever they can find.

We have many of the same animals found across the continent: rats, mice, skunks, raccoons, foxes, possums, bats, ants, termites, gophers, moles, hawks, and others. They're tolerable until they begin to pillage and destroy, and then we have to take action. In this ongoing dance, I've learned, through trial and error, some effective methods of dealing with the invaders.

Rats and Mice

They've been part of the human equation from time immemorial and are survivors par excellence. (If we humans succeed in eliminating life on Earth, there'll still be rats and cockroaches — and pampas grass and Scotch broom.)

Rodents are immensely clever and adaptable, amazing in their ability to delicately remove food from a trap without springing it.

Maybe two or three times a year, mice get into the pantry, where they'll chew open packages of nuts or grains and leave telltale pellets.

I use standard traps, never poison; poison makes an animal die from internal bleeding — cruel and unusual punishment. When there is evidence of rodent activity, I generally set three to five traps, either on vertical walls (screwed on) or horizontal passages (after a while, you figure out their routes).

Kness Snap-E Rat Trap; there are smaller ones of the same design for mice.
shltr.net/hah11

They did make a better mouse (rat) trap, and this is it. You fill the container with peanut butter, cheese, etc. and the rat will generally trigger the (very strong) spring when it tries to pry out the food. Use gloves when setting any traps, so there won't be any human smell on the traps.

I screw the trap down. If I don't, another rat (or raccoon or fox) may carry off the trap with the rat for a midnight snack.

Rat Facts

Rats breed at three to four months of age, and can produce up to seven litters a year, each containing 10 to 20 babies. It's said that there are as many rats in the United States as humans. More than 1,000 rats per acre were reported on one Iowa farm, and one rat can eat about 50 pounds of grain a year.

Country rats are a lot different from city rats. The former are vegetarians and they're clean little animals for the most part. They look like an oversized mouse, with big eyes, big ears, and soft fur. City rats are another story. I've seen skuzzy yellow-fanged rats scurrying around on the sidewalks and vacant lots in New York City that gave me nightmares.

Dusky-footed woodrats (also known as packrats) build conical 3'-high, 3'-diameter structures (twig high-rises), always in a dense part of the woods away from paths or roads. These constructions are architecturally complex, with many rooms, some serving as lookouts, others as pantries for food storage.

Woodrat nest

Bats

We had bats in our belfry. We sleep in the second story of a three-story tower, and bats were living in infinitesimally small cracks in the third-story ceiling and then occasionally swooping down into our bedroom, looking for a way out.

We'd wake up to the swish of wings, I'd open the windows, and a bat would swoop out into the night. Shades of Dracula!

Our tower is covered with hand-split shakes, so there are small crevices under the eaves. I found every crack I could and covered them with quarter-inch mesh. They still got in, so I got some industrial grade foam and shot it into every inside and outside crack I could find. Finally, after several years of intermittent bat encounters, they were gone (from inside) altogether.

Don't get me wrong, I'm an admirer of bats. They're beautifully designed, with elegant membrane-webbed wings. They use a type of sonar called echolocation, bouncing signals off objects in front of them, enabling them to fly in the dark. Plus, they eat tons of insects. But they can get through unbelievably small spaces. If you can poke a pencil through a crack, don't be surprised if a bat can wiggle through.

For more information on bats, including do-it-yourself bat exclusion techniques, a nationwide listing of professional "bat excluders," or simply how to live in harmony with them, visit Bat Conservation International:

www.batcon.org

Gophers

My neighbor, a knowledgeable botanist, swears by the Black Hole Rodent Trap, which its manufacturer claims is the number one selling gopher trap in the United States.

Black Hole Spring-Loaded Gopher Trap
shltr.net/hah12

Macabee Trap
shltr.net/hah13

I use Macabee traps, the old-fashioned, hard-to-set type. When we see a lettuce or artichoke plant disappear, I gingerly dig around with a shovel to find the gopher's tunnel(s). I put on light cloth gloves to mask my scent and dig back into the tunnel with a trowel. I set the trap, gently push it into the tunnel (pincers of trap facing gopher direction), and then put some lettuce or other vegetable behind the trap so they'll get nailed if they come after it. I then push dirt in to cover up the tunnel.

I have a string attached to the trap, tied to a wooden stake, and driven into the ground. I leave the string loose on the ground. When it's pulled taut, I know I've got a gopher. If you don't do this, they'll occasionally retreat to unreachable subterranean depths and you'll never find the trap. An even better method is to find a main tunnel and set traps going in both directions.

Possums

The only time I've gone after possums was when a bunch of them began to shit all over my lumber storage area. They're easy to trap. I caught 13 of them in a few months, in the same Havahart trap I use for skunks, took them a few miles away and released them. For some reason, in recent years, there are no possums around here.

Possums will sometimes bare their teeth, hiss or even growl, appearing to be fierce, but they will seldom fight and are rarely aggressive.

Playing possum: One night when I was closing in the chickens, I spotted a baby possum. As soon as it saw me, it rolled over on its side, closed its eyes and lay still, with occasional peeks to see if I'd gone away. It made me laugh out loud.

Raccoons

We generally coexist with raccoons. You never want to have your dogs take one on, though, because you'll end up with an eviscerated canine. Raccoons are ferocious fighters, and clever, too. Years ago, one of them pulled the recirculating pump out of our fishpond, which drained it, and proceeded to feast on the stranded carp.

The one raccoon I trapped had climbed in the studio window and left messy paw prints all over my desk. I also put quarter-inch mesh or chicken wire about a foot down in the ground all around the chicken coop so raccoons and skunks can't tunnel into their yard at night.

I use a #1050 Havahart Large Raccoon trap #3A. There are 10 different sizes of Havahart traps; you'll find them online at the Havahart website, and at most lawn and garden stores. I tie the bait to the trigger inside the trap.

www.havahart.com

Skunks

I only trap skunks if they persist in blasting our environs, or manage to kill chickens. Most of the time, I'm happy to have them around; they are beautiful little animals. But when the need arises, be careful. Skunks can make your life miserable.

Skunks have poor eyesight. If you're sitting in the garden or standing still in the woods and a skunk comes ambling along, they may come quite close without bothering you. Just don't make any sudden moves.

A skunk can shoot its spray as far as 12 feet, and it is said that it will aim for another animal's eyes.

Note that a skunk has to raise its tail to spray, so keep the tail down if at all possible. Use a trap small enough for skunks to get into, but not high enough for it to raise its tail.

When you get a skunk in a Havahart trap, throw a blanket or tarp over the trap while you plan what to do; the darkness will quiet the skunk down. A friend of mine loads the traps into the back of his pickup truck and releases them four miles out in the countryside.

If you get skunked: A popular method for neutralizing skunk spray is to scrub yourself with a mixture of 1 quart hydrogen peroxide, ⅓ cup baking soda, and 1 tablespoon liquid soap. Leave it on for a minute, then wash it off.

By the way, baby skunks are absolutely the cutest animals I've ever seen. They're miniatures of big skunks.

I use this Havahart trap for skunks. It's 10˝ by 11˝ by 36˝.

Hawks

A young, red-shouldered hawk was picking off our chickens, so in our most recently built chicken coop, we stretched aviary wire over their yard, which worked perfectly.

One day, years ago, a hawk got trapped in the chicken yard just as guests appeared. They watched as I netted the hawk and let it go.

Termites

Just about all the homes in my small town get dry-wood termite damage at one time or another. Formerly you had a choice between methyl bromide (thankfully now banned) and Vikane fumigant —a Dow product—need to know anything more? The home gets tented, you move out for 24 hours, they fumigate, you move back in.

I would never do this. If it's going to kill termites several inches inside the wood, I don't believe that there will be no residue or eventual ill effects.

These days there are a bunch of non-toxic treatments: orange or Neem oil, borates, the Electrogun (fries them with 90,000 volts), parasitic nematodes, etc. Trouble is, it will cost you a few thousand dollars, and you'll probably have to do it over in several years.

For 10 or so years I've been using a cedar oil spray *(at right)*. When I see termite frass (pellets) that have dropped from the ceiling, I spray this stuff on the area. It smells good, and I don't know why or how, but it works. No more termites, at least for years. (You'd think that application on the surface wouldn't be sufficient, but it seems to be.)

www.greenbugallnatural.com

Ants

Years ago, we had a really bad infestation of ants. We solved the problem by going to ***www.bugspray.com***, which has a very complete list of solutions for controlling pests. Since that time, we've been able to control ants by using Terro Liquid Ant Baits, widely available, where the main ingredient is Borax—a natural mineral.

Conclusion on Pests

In these never-ending battles, I've come to realize that our stay on the land is temporary at best. We're just fending off the natural forces for a while. When we're gone, they'll take over. When humans are gone, there will still be rats, cockroaches, Eucalyptus trees, pampas grass, and Scotch broom.

The Shop

The first shop I built became what is now our production studio. Then I built a very simple 14′ by 20′ shed roof structure with a concrete slab floor. Funny, it's at the northern end of our property, facing south, and in retrospect would have been the best site for the house.

The shop is stuffed with tools and materials I've gathered over the years.

In the back is an outdoor work area, and my "corporation yard," where lumber, pipe, and plywood are stacked in racks — a solution to having a small area.

For all these years, I've saved nuts, bolts, and washers, and just about anything that might be useful some day. I got into doing this when I lived in Big Sur, an hour's drive on winding roads to the closest lumber yards and hardware stores, and I couldn't just run down to the store and get a needed item.

Outdoors, rear of shop: "corporation yard'

Stacking lumber due to small space

Shop Tools

I'm showing some, not all, of my tools; When I started on these pages, I kept running out to the shop to shoot more photos. I had to quit before half this book was on tools. For example, I'm not showing plumbing, wiring, caulking, roofing, or painting tools.

I'm amazed at how many I've acquired. But then again, this is over a 60-year period.

Saws

OK, so I'm with saws as Imelda Marcos was with shoes. Here they are:

Table saw A Delta, I got this used about eight years ago (to replace a Bosch Gravity-Rise Worksite portable table saw, which burned out, was unfixable, and I do not recommend).

Makita chop saw
Lew gave me this old saw; I had it fixed (for some $200). It'll cut through 4×4s. It also allows for great accuracy in cross-cutting, because you can  place the blade down on the wood to check before cutting.

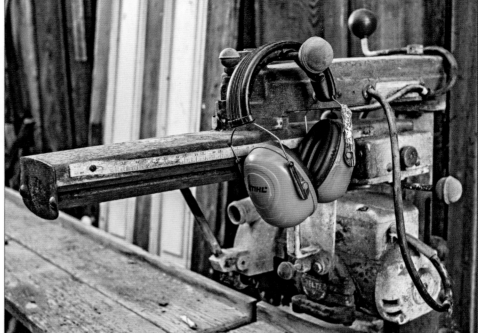

Radial arm saw I'm fond of radial arm saws. It was the first tool I learned to use when I got a job as a carpenter on the San Francisco docks at age 18. I bought this old beauty secondhand some 40 years ago from a lady whose husband had passed away. American made, it's still working fine.

Skilsaw I've always like this type of circular saw as opposed to the heavier worm-drive circular saw, mainly because I can operate it with one hand.

Grizzly bandsaw
Inexpensive, a Grizzly tool. Works great.

***www.grizzly.com/
woodworking-bandsaws***

Sawzall (below) Made by Milwaukee Electric Tool Co., this is a reciprocating saw used by construction workers, electricians, wreckers, drywall applicators, etc. The design hasn't changed in 50 years.

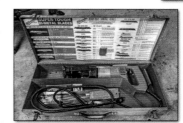

142

Old-fashioned bow saw I used this back in the day for cutting curves. You turn the blade to get a curve as you cut.

Makita jigsaw I got this recently, one of those tools I wish I'd had all along. I use it instead of the bow saw (*see above*) these days.

Japanese hand saws When I saw that Canadian builder Bruno Atkey (see *Builders of the Pacific Coast*) had put aside his American saws for Japanese saws, I did the same. A completely different approach to sawing. These saws cut on the pull, rather than the push. I can get a more accurate starting cut, and a more accurate overall cut.

www.japanwoodworker.com

Some of my hand saws
From top left:

Stanley Fat Max hand saw — a unique saw, cuts quickly and well, good for rough work;

Old Disston rip saw;

Mini keyhole saw;

Tenon saw;

Sharksaw pull saw (black handle);

Another tenon saw (orange handle);

Regular keyhole saw

Chainsaw I've had this 24″ Stihl MS 270 for 15 years. It's been a critical tool for years: firewood, trimming trees, cutting up redwood to split into shakes, etc. It still runs fine. Every time I use it, I sharpen the teeth before putting it away.

Note: Chainsaws are dangerous. I highly recommend a helmet like this, which provides protection for your head, a face guard, and ear protectors.

Makita cordless driver drill and impact driver This set came with a great flashlight, two 18-volt batteries, and a charger. Every one of these units is outstanding. Impact drivers are a revelation to me.

shltr.net/hah14

Makita corded ½" drill I wanted something more powerful than my portable Makita drill, so got this. I buy as many tools as I can at local, employee-owned, Jackson's Hardware in San Rafael, California; they have knowledgeable people there to consult, something you're not going to find at Amazon. It's worth it to pay a little more for the good advice.

Crooked knife Used by First Nations totem carvers and other Native American tribes for carving, hollowing out bowls, a multitude of uses. About $90 from *www.kestreltool.com*

Grizzly belt/disc sander I use this a lot, both the belt and the disc. Grizzly has a full line of tools, all reliable, inexpensive.

www.grizzly.com/sanders

Tenon cutter This tool makes round tenons for rustic furniture, as shown below. There is a corresponding bit for each cutter to drill the right size hole for that cutter.

www.northerntool.com/shop/tools/category_tenon-cutters-kits

Small Stanley block plane One of my favorite tools. I used it extensively when building, mostly to take edges off boards, like, say, exposed rafters. It's a little trick that highlights the wood, especially with weathered and/or used wood.

shltr.net/hah15

Makita Random orbit sander I keep this portable sander handy to the outdoor work area and grab it often.

shltr.net/hah16

Foredom rotary tool This is like an upgraded Dremel. It can be used for many purposes; it has hundreds of attachments. Mine has a flexible shaft and is operated with a foot pedal. I use it a lot for sanding off rust with sandpaper flap wheels, and for carving letters in wood. It's a tool used extensively by jewelers.

www.foredom.net

Ear guards I never use a power tool without these ear guards. Thanks to Paul Wingate for turning me on to safety equipment in the '60s.

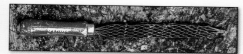

Japanese saw rasp This is one of those Japanese "ah-hah" tools. It's made of 10 saw blades joined together in a diamond pattern. It removes wood aggressively, yet leaves a relatively smooth surface.

shltr.net/hah17

Nail pullers from top:

- Crescent nail puller, miraculous tool for pulling sunk-in nails with minimum wood scarring
- SuperBar: thin, flexible, for getting into tight cracks
- Crowbar: superior design. I don't see these online anywhere. I got mine (two sizes) at Jackson's Hardware in San Rafael, California.
- Japanese cat's paw, for prying up heads of flush nails

Tool belt Carpenters will be amused, but I still use this old-fashioned tool belt. Hammer, tape measure, Kleyn pliers, regular and Phillips screwdrivers, combination square, two nail punches, pencil, two chisels. In the pouches: 6d, 8d, and 16d hot-dipped galvanized nails.

Honda 3000 Inverter Generator Super-quiet. Excellent machine. Expensive (costs three times now what I paid for it 10 years ago). We use it to keep the office running during power outages.

Carving hatchet I can't remember where I got this. It doesn't have a name on it, just an etched drawing of what looks like a moose. It's used by spoon makers for roughing out. It's a joy to use. I try to get all my builder friends to try it out.

Three hatchets (L-R)
Estwing hatchet for splitting kindling;
Japanese carpenter's hatchet;
Shingling hatchet

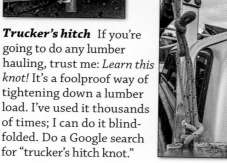

Trucker's hitch If you're going to do any lumber hauling, trust me: *Learn this knot!* It's a foolproof way of tightening down a lumber load. I've used it thousands of times; I can do it blindfolded. Do a Google search for "trucker's hitch knot."

Pickup truck I've had maybe half a dozen pickup trucks (including a 1937 Chevy with square-cut gears). My current truck is a 2003 Toyota Tacoma 4×4, stick shift, 5-speed, 4-cylinder model that is a dependable workhorse (in all these years, it has never failed to start). It's not only great for camping, but for building. I have an aluminum *Hauler rack* (**www.haulerracks.com**) that rests on the truck bed rails (not on the camper shell) and can carry 1,200 pounds. The rack comes to you via UPS, and you assemble it and bolt it to the truck.

Ladders Two ladders of note here:

1. At left, the wooden ladder with the single leg in the middle is a pruning ladder that has been in my family for 70 years.
2. Next to it, the aluminum Little Giant multi-use ladder is a masterpiece of design. It can be configured into a bunch of different forms — stepladders or extension ladders. A tool I wish I'd had decades ago.

www.littlegiantladder.com

Skins and Bones

Roadkill (*n*): Animals killed by vehicles on roads

Every state has different roadkill regulations. In California, it is technically illegal to pick up any roadkill, but there is currently a bill in the California Senate that will allow people to pick up deer, elk, antelope, and wild pigs, as long as they apply for a free permit within 24 hours.

There are now 20 states that allow picking up roadkill animals, including Washington, Colorado, Georgia, Idaho, Illinois, Indiana, Maryland, New Hampshire, North Dakota, New York, Ohio, Pennsylvania, Tennessee, and several others. Some of these states require permits.

Most of the talk about roadkill refers to deer, but there are many other smaller animals that get hit by cars: raccoons, skunks, foxes, bobcats, weasels, squirrels, etc. You are not taking the animal's life; it's already dead.

Roadkill is a win-win-win situation. There's a beautiful skin, a skull, and sometimes meat. With the meat factor, you are getting fresh organic wild protein and avoiding the chemicals and pollution caused by the production of hay and grain for beef cattle.

There's a bluegrass song, "Why would anyone eat beef when he can have squirrel?"

At the same time, picking up roadkill avoids having rotting animals on the roadside.

My collection here is partly passed down from my family (before there were California restrictions), and animals I found in traveling through states that allow roadkill retrieval. Several of the bobcats are from farmers who had permits; the bobcats were killing their chickens.

Check out the regulations in your state.

Skins

- Check out YouTube videos for technique. Also, if you get *The Small Mammal Manual Manuscript* (*see next page*), it has a page on skinning with good step-by-step instructions.

- Skin the animal, getting as much flesh off as you can.

- Lay the skin out, fur side down, on a piece of plywood, pinning it with push pin, stretching it as tightly as possible.

- Cover it completely with salt, so no skin is showing.

- In about a week, remove the salt and deliver it (or ship it off) to a tannery. (Or you can tan it yourself — something I've never tried.)

Note on skunks (which have beautiful glossy skins): Once in a while, a skunk will get hit on the head and die before releasing its smell. In skinning, you just have to steer way clear of the oil gland next to the anus.

Skin from 4′ rattlesnake found on road at San Juanico (Scorpion Bay), Baja California. There are 12 segments on the rattles. (This doesn't mean the snake is 12 years old.)

Skinning knives (L–R):

Geisser Rostfrei 3000 18. I like this for skinning deer. Huge selection of knives at: **www.2order1.com/giesserknives**

Spyderco Moran 3⅞″ Drop Point Knife, a beautiful, balanced hunting knife (about $100): **shltr.net/hah18**

Havalon Piranta Edge knife with interchangeable blades. I like this better than the popular Wyoming knives: **www.havalon.com/piranta-fitment-2**

Homemade tool for scooping brains out of skulls after boiling; made from thick wire, bent, then flattened at one end on anvil

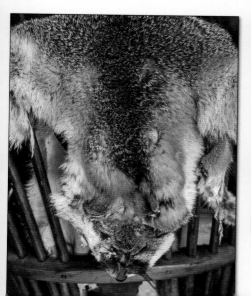

Left, grey fox (I generally try to save the nose, ears, and whiskers). Above, skin of a roadkill fawn on back of chair

L–R: Two bear skulls from British Columbia; beaver skull found on a lake on Denman Island, BC — note length of two teeth; four bobcat skulls; a bunch of fox skulls; small ones in front are weasel and rat skulls

Far right: Dog skull found in Rocky Mountains near Palmer Lake, Colorado (while out running in the snow with my friend Bob Anderson, author of Stretching)

Bones

I always try to keep the skull. Kids are invariably fascinated by them.

First you boil it to get the meat off, then scoop out the brain *(see tool on previous page)*. Next, use strong ammonia to remove grease and then strong hydrogen peroxide to bleach it.

Books on Skins and Bones

The Small Mammal Manual Manuscript by Lee Post

This is a unique homemade book with great drawings. "A step-by-step guide to preparing and articulating small mammal skeletons"

shltr.net/hah19

Skulls and Bones by Glen Searfoss

A good, basic book that identifies mammal skulls and bones

shltr.net/hah20

Animal Skulls: A Guide to North American Species by Mark Elbroch

A very complete book on the subject. I ordered a copy after looking through Amazon's "Look Inside the Book."

shltr.net/hah21

Van Dyke's Taxidermy Catalog

All things taxidermic. How about a "Reproduction White Rhinoceros" for $9,895.00? Check out the less exotic stuff and useful tools of the trade:

www.vandykestaxidermy.com

Two bobcat skulls

Left: Cattle skull from arroyo in Baja California Sur; Right: Horse skull found at Diana's Punch Bowl, near Austin, Nevada

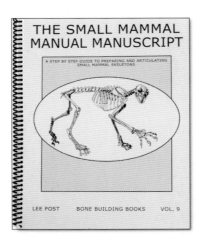

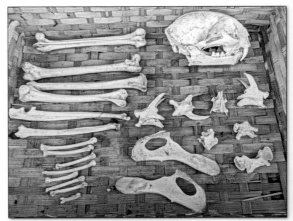

Bones from bobcat found in woods

When I was a kid, I wanted to be a taxidermist. I sent away $5 for a year's subscription to *Modern Taxidermist* magazine, which advertised "money-making taxidermic methods." I was fascinated then (as now) by the art and craft of taxidermy.

Various bird skulls

Barn owl in a field. Exquisite. I had to leave it there, since it's illegal to possess an owl. At least I have a photo.

Three mummies. Found little fish on beach; I forget where I found the mouse (kids love it); bat got trapped in greenhouse and died.

Appendix
Advice to Someone Building a Home

I wrote this letter to homeowners whose homes were destroyed in the Santa Rosa, Californira fire of October 2017. It summarizes what I've learned in over 50 years of building.

I would like to offer some suggestions to people whose homes were destroyed by the California fires of 2017. I've built three homes of my own and been publishing books on building for some 45 years and have come to some conclusions about practical, sensible building.

Much of the emphasis in our books has been on owner-building, and if you will be doing design and construction yourself, these are things for you to consider. If not, these are ideas you can discuss with architects and/or builders you may be working with — the principles are the same.

Much has been learned about building homes in the last two or three decades. You may be able to take advantage of building materials and techniques that weren't available when these homes were built. Here is a chance to do things better, to learn from experience, to create a home built from sustainable materials that will save energy, that will be better for you and the planet.

Please note: *These are just random ideas for your consideration. This isn't a checklist, where you try to incorporate each suggestion in your plans. The purpose here is to stimulate thinking. Maybe you'll find two or three ideas that will work for you.*

- Consider putting a tiny home on the site for a temporary place to live. You can get one ready-made, and I recommend the ones built by Ward Hensill in Bodega: ***www.bodegaportablebuildings.com***

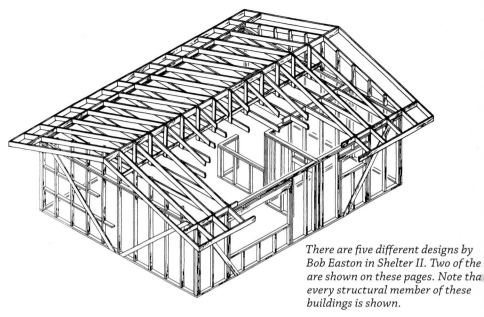

There are five different designs by Bob Easton in Shelter II. Two of the are shown on these pages. Note tha every structural member of these buildings is shown.

OR get a Tuff Shed: You prepare the foundation/floor, and they erect the building in one day. You then finish the interior: ***www.tuffshed.com***

OR for a local (Petaluma) manufacturer of small (not tiny) homes: Stephen Marshall at ***www.littlehouseonthetrailer.com***

- If you build a tiny (or small) house first, it can later be a guest house, studio, or "granny flat."

- Consider some sort of pre-fab starting point to get the house framed up quickly and ready for services and finishing.

- For example, some friends in Carpinteria had the shell of their house steel-framed by local barn builders. They carried on and completed the finishing themselves, but the fire-resistant shell went up in a few days.

- Consider the orientation of your property. Windows facing south will allow for solar heating. Deciduous trees can be planted so there is shade in the summer, sun in the winter (when trees are bare). What direction do the winds/storms come from? Where does the sun rise and set at various times of the year?

- Consider having a large-enough section of the roof sloping and facing direct south for maximization of solar panels (which can be added years later).

- Have the home built in two stages. Get the kitchen/bathroom/living/sleeping areas done first, with plans to add on later, so you can live there ASAP.

- Even if you hire a builder, do some of the work yourself. I built most of a house in the '60s by working on weekends, after work, and holidays. You can save a lot of money by doing some of the simple stuff.

- Stud frame construction. Straw bale, cob, timber frame, and other natural materials each have their benefits, but the stud wall system, with insulation, wiring, and plumbing within the walls is by far the quickest way to build.

- Rectangular design. Stick with rectangles. If you get into building curves, or polygons (*e.g.*, hexagonal, octagonal) you'll end up spending a lot more time and money.

- Use Class A roofing materials, which are "effective against severe fire test exposures."

- Consider Hardie board fiber cement siding for exterior walls. It's a cement fiber product that looks like wood, but will not rot, and is fire-resistant, insect-resistant, impact-resistant, and moisture-resistant.

- Use some kind of non-toxic insulation (not available when I built), such as wool, denim, and cellulose made from recycled paper products. Research it. "Roxul" is a very good non-toxic, non-water–absorbing, non-rodent- and non-insect–supporting type of batt insulation.

How can you waste less in your new home?

- Have a central core, including kitchen/bathroom back-to-back (for plumbing simplicity).

- Consider wearing layers of winter warmth rather than keeping the entire house at 70 degrees. We wear 4 to 5 layers of cotton, wool, and down in the winter; it feels good and lessens energy consumption for heating.

- Locate the hot water heater in a central core area, including a wood (or gas) stove for space heating, with a coil for heating water in winter, plus a solar-heated water panel on the roof for summer hot water.

- Consider a small 5-gallon electric hot water heater under the kitchen sink. We have one, and it provides almost instant hot water, with no waiting, and doesn't use much electricity.

- Consider facing your kitchen south. I'd get the kitchen floor as low as possible (concrete slab with stringers, plywood, then linoleum). (Don't have a wooden floor in the kitchen if you really cook; linoleum is easy to clean.) The reason for the low floor is so that you easily step out to:

  a) An outdoor cooking/eating area with a roof, right outside the kitchen. Weber barbecue, table, sink. This is cheap square footage, and you can do a lot of cooking, eating, and socializing outdoors in warmer weather.

  b) A vegetable garden easily accessible to the kitchen

- Don't install a kitchen-sink garbage disposal unit. It's a bad practice to grind up food, especially if it's going to a septic tank. Rather, compost kitchen scraps using a compost-ing tumbler.

- Consider washing dishes by hand; don't install a dishwasher. Here's a video of my technique: ***shltr.net/dishwashing***

- Have a window at the kitchen sink, so you can look outside while doing dishes.

- Install a BlueStar range (made in America) if you are serious about cooking. The one we have has no digital controls. It cost $3100 and is one of the best things we've ever bought.

- Consider getting a tank to collect rainwater off the roof.

- Set up valves to divert greywater for wash basin, bath, and shower.

- If you are interested in gardening, in providing some of your own food, consider where a vegetable garden might best be located.

- Plant some fruit and/or shade trees. (If I was starting over again, I'd plant half a dozen olive trees.)

- Avoid architectural cleverness. Watch out for architects trying to make a statement. Quite often, tried and true designs produce economical, practical homes. The wheel needn't be reinvented.

- Wire your house for internet access. (This step may be eliminated if you are satisfied with wireless speeds, but wired connections can be faster.)

- Set up automatic backups of your computer, smartphone, iPad, and other digital devices on the Cloud. Also, back up all photos on the Cloud; you can set up your smartphone to automatically back up all photos you shoot. This way, all your data will be saved even if the devices are destroyed in a fire (or stolen or lost).

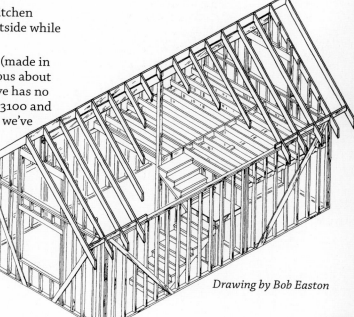

Drawing by Bob Easton

Learning to Build

I'm often asked about learning the craft of carpentry. There are schools in various parts of the country, like Yestermorrow in Warren, Vermont, or The North House Folk School in Grand Marais, Minnesota, where you can take courses in timber frame construction. I'm sure that in searching around on the Internet, you can find many other opportunities to learn the skills of building.

On-the-job training But I also tell people what I learned from my friend Paul Wingate in the '60s. Paul went around to building sites and talked to the contractors or carpenters. He wanted to learn carpentry and he offered to clean up, carry materials, or help out in any way, free of charge.

He got a job right away, and swept the floors, carried lumber and sheet rock, and looked around to see how he could help the carpenters. Pretty soon he was cutting 2×4s for them, handing them tools he saw they needed. Right away, he began learning building skills, and pretty soon he started getting paid. Paul turned out to be a highly skilled carpenter, and it all started this way.

Can you do it? If you've ever worked with your hands — gardening, crafts, sewing, soldering — you can most likely learn to build. If you've never done anything with your hands, you can still probably learn enough carpentry to build a house.

How to start On the first day of building my first house, I asked my friend and helper Bob what to do. He picked up

Maso Finiguerra (1426–64), Apprentice Woodworker, Uffizi, Florence

a pick, started digging the foundation trench, and said: "This."

From that point on, I've known that to get started, I just have to…start. Simple, and true. A lot of times I'm not sure what to do, but the momentum of starting causes me to focus and figure it out.

I'm not saying this is for everyone. Some people will figure it all out in advance, and it will go well. But the above method — my lifetime M.O. — of starting when I don't have it all mapped out, will work for a lot of people.

To get going right away One way to start a building project right now, if you have no experience, would be to hire a carpenter, and work along with him in building the house, learning as you go. You can also learn a lot from books, which I referred to constantly while building.

Beware of making your house a trip
All too many first-time owner-builders underestimate the value of simplicity and practicality in building. It's happened to me twice. The first time, it was a beautiful architect-designed plan, that was beyond my abilities. The second time, it was the abstract concept of building geodesic domes. *(See both of these projects on p. 159.)* In fact, even the post-and-beam structures I worked on did not have the simplicity that I finally arrived at with rectangular stud-frame construction.

This method isn't for everyone, but it's what works for me, in my part of the world, with northern California climate and locally available materials. I concluded that I wanted to get a house up and running — certainly to have it aesthetically pleasing — but to have it functioning for the life we wanted to lead, and not to take forever to finish.

Robert Venable, a experienced carpenter I interviewed in *Shelter*, said this about a house being a trip: "The house is just a garment. You don't spend your life knitting a sweater. You need the sweater, you knit it, you put it on…and now you look at the world."

Could You Do This Nowadays?

Yes, with qualifications:

Building on a piece of land In the '60s, it was a common goal to find land on which to build a home. This was the icon of '60s owner-building — the hippie dream — the country homestead.

Today, you probably can't find land (at a reasonable price) within an hour or so of any large city in North America on which to build your own home. But there are alternatives: buying land out in the country, or looking for small homes that can be fixed up in towns or cities.

Fixing up an old house is an alternative to starting from scratch. If I intended to build my own home now, and didn't want to start on a bare piece of land, I'd look for an old home in a town (or city) that needed fixing up. I'd have the advantage of water, sewage, and power already in place, and not have to start from the ground up.

Examples of fixer-uppers Friends of ours bought a repossessed home in a small town in Oregon for $112,000 two years ago, and have now fixed it up completely.

A family bought a run-down 1,100 square-foot home on a hillside in Los Angeles for about $200,000, fixed the

rotten floors and disintegrating foundation, and now have a happy home in one of the most expensive cities in the country. (*See pp. 178–181, Small Homes.*)

In San Francisco, two families bought a home and (with permits), turned it into a duplex — cutting their initial costs in half (*pp. 174–177, Small Homes*).

In Oakland, California, a young cabinetmaker lives in a small studio he has created adjacent to his shop in an industrial area. Rent: $250 per month.

In Victoria, BC, Canada, a young surfer/storeowner lives in a school bus parked on a lot in the industrial part of the city.

These are a few creative alternatives to building a home on a piece of land in the country.

Cost Everything was much cheaper in the '70s. Our half-acre was $6,500, the building permit $200. It was OK to build with used materials. I drew up my own plans, and was my own architect and engineer.

Now, building permits have become complex, demanding, and highly expensive. All the permits here (Marin County, California), including the California Coastal Development permit, amount to over $50,000 for a new home.

Our gravity-powered septic system cost about $3,000. The complex systems now required in Marin County are between $50,000 and $80,000.

But away from the expensive metropolitan areas, it's a different matter. Land is more affordable in the country, codes less demanding, and building a home is still possible.

Time In building three homes over the years, I found that working full time and alone, it took roughly a year to build a house, even if the finish work wasn't complete.

If you could save up enough money for a year's living expenses, you could work full time on a house (and then get on with your life).

If you decide to build a home, or fix up an old one, this will be the main thing you'll be doing in your life. You won't be spending a lot of time watching sports, or eating out, or going on vacations to tropical countries. You won't be spending a lot of time on Facebook or Instagram either.

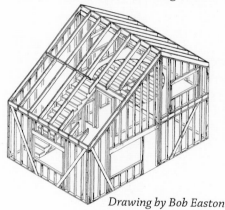

Drawing by Bob Easton

You'll be pouring the foundation, nailing down the subfloor, putting on the siding and roofing, figuring out how to do things you've probably never done before.

Getting help You might not do everything yourself. You might subcontract out plumbing, wiring, roofing, or get carpentry help. For each owner-builder, it will be different.

The '60s

Anti-Vietnam War parade, New York City, September, 1956

This page on what went on in North America in the '60s is here because so much of what we did in building and gardening and crafts, as shown in these pages, was influenced by concepts of the '60s, by tools and thoughts and practices publicized in the *Whole Earth Catalog* and by a large underground network of do-it-yourself, like-minded people.

As the '70s evolved from the '60s, so did the '50s set the stage for the '60s.

The '50s

Affluent times The '50s was a time of plenty. There were jobs, with benefits; unions were strong. The GI Bill allowed veterans to go to college or buy a house. People bought large homes in the suburbs, along with labor-saving appliances. Auto production surged.

Note: The good times were not enjoyed by everyone, but certainly by a significant majority of white, middle-class Americans.

The "baby boom," referring to the population growth that occurred between 1946–1964, with its peak in 1957, added 50 million babies by the end of the 1950s; it was the highest birthrate in American history, and concurrently the biggest generational transfer of wealth in our country's history.

Consumerism It turned out to be an era of consumerism. American factories went from robust wartime manufacturing to a booming production of consumer goods; it was an era of unprecedented material prosperity.

Conformity Concurrently, it evolved into an era of conformity.

The Man in a Grey Flannel Suit by Sloan Wilson, written in 1956, was about conformity and the struggle of an individual to escape devotion to material culture.

The Organization Man by William H. Whyte, published in 1956, depicted the empty life of people working for corporations, who sacrificed individuality for corporate safety.

Enter the '60s

Catalysts for change When the baby boom generation grew up, many of them rejected material success and its accompanying conformity, and sought other avenues in life and means of expression. It's hard to believe, but all the following ideas, concepts, perceptions, movements, arts, practices, discoveries, and acts were going on in the '60s:

Zen Buddhism, meditation, the Tarot, the Kabbalah, the I Ching, martial arts, women's liberation, gay rights, the sexual revolution, black power, Native American culture, marijuana and LSD, political activism, building your own house, organic gardening and farming, revival of crafts, alternative energy sources: sun, wind, and water, organic gardening and farming, ecological awareness, self-sufficiency, the Beat poets, the blues and rock 'n' roll, the Beatles, the Rolling Stones, Bob Dylan, *Rolling Stone* magazine and dozens of new underground newspapers, dolphin consciousness, viewing the earth from space, *The Whole Earth Catalog*, planetary consciousness, whole systems, the West Coast publishing revolution, the first desktop computers, domes, long hair, new styles of dressing, the Human Be-In, the Monterey Pop Festival . . .

Note: Many of these things were not so much new, as they were new to this very large group of young people — who had the time and means to study and experiment — and set out on new courses in their lives.

All of these things were part of our world in the '60s, and carried over into what we did in the '70s, including building this homestead.

Reality Check

I've done here what I've always done in my photography: picked the best angles, the best lighting, the most complimentary colors (although we're showing the house in its day-to-day operation, rather than staging things as do magazines and books on architecture).

This is looking at our world through a rose-colored lens. It's our best foot forward, but it's not necessarily an accurate picture of the day-to-day work and the constant maintenance and fixing stuff that's part of running a homestead. We have too many projects and not enough time, but we wouldn't want it otherwise.

"Before enlightenment, chop wood, carry water;
after enlightenment, chop wood, carry water."

–Zen saying

Building Experience

I'm describing my experience with building because it relates to the work I did on this, my final house.

Concrete Block House in Colusa

When I was 12, I helped my dad build a house in Colusa, California (in the Sacramento Valley). We worked on weekends and vacations. It was a concrete block house with a poured concrete slab floor, and my job was shoveling sand, gravel, and cement into a concrete mixer and then wheelbarrowing it to the house.

1947. My dad and me testing the first water from our well in Colusa

One day, after the walls and floor were done and the roof framed, they gave me a carpenter's apron and a hammer, and let me nail down the roof sheathing. Boy, did I like that! The sweet smell of the wood, the satisfaction of hammering nails in, the feeling of accomplishment once the job was done. I was hooked — I liked building.

When I was 18, I got a union job working for a shipwright on the docks in San Francisco. (This was in the early '50s, and San Francisco was still a major west-coast port.) Our job was to go on board the cargo ships once they were loaded, and build frameworks in the holds to secure the cargo. When there were no ships in town, we would rebuild pallets in our yard down at the foot of Hyde Street. I made $2.50 per hour, double-time for overtime, which was a great wage for the times.

Building in Mill Valley

Flash forward to 1960 — my wife Sarah and I bought a half-acre piece of land in Mill Valley with a summer house and two small cabins. My first building was converting the carport into a sod roof (now called "living roof") studio.

My next project was an ambitious remodel of the summer house. One of my surfing friends, John Stonum, was in his last year of architectural school at UC Berkeley and designed a concrete and timber structure. Looking back on it now, I can see that it was far more complex than it could have been, but *c'est la vie.*

I was working as an insurance broker in San Francisco at the time, and I'd rush home from work each night and work until dark, and work on the weekends and holidays. I got the house about two-thirds finished.

1961. My first building project, a studio with living roof in Mill Valley, California

1963–65. Main house on Mill Valley property. These concrete walls were 12´ high. In pouring the walls, I used rough-sawn Douglas fir form boards vertically so the grain pattern showed in the finished concrete. I made the shakes from an old-growth deadfall tree in the Mendocino woods.

Rancho Rico

In 1965, when the countercultural revolution was well underway, I quit my job as an insurance broker in San Francisco and went to work as a carpenter. In 1966 I got a job as foreman on a job in Big Sur, building a large house overlooking the ocean out of massive bridge timbers. The site was on a 400-acre ranch, formerly a chicken farm. There were two private beaches on the land.

We moved down there and remodeled a chicken coop to live in while I worked on the house. It took three of us about a year to get the building's complex foundation poured and the timber framing complete.

For the main beams of the house, we spliced together two 16´-long, 8×22 timbers, each unit weighing about 500 pounds. Luckily for us, the ranch foreman, Ted Garr, rigged up a boom on the back of a backhoe, to lift the beams into place.

Rancho Rico: Main framing completed

ting 8×22 redwood posts with tractor boom

157

Burns Creek

I quit the job at that point; it was no longer what I wanted to be doing, and I then built my own home at Burns Creek in Big Sur, about two miles north of Esalen.

All the wood was recycled, except for the floor and roof decking, which was Monterey pine from Carmel Valley. The siding was used lumber from a farm labor camp I tore down in Salinas and the exterior was covered with shakes I split from short pieces of old-growth redwood that had been left in the woods by loggers.

As opposed to the house in Mill Valley and the bridge timber house in Big Sur, I was my own architect here, and my aim was simplicity.

The house was a large shed. Both the floor girders and roof beams consisted of 30′ long rough Douglas fir lumber that had been salvaged from an old horse stable in San Francisco. The 14 posts were 12′-long, 4×12 (double-track) redwood railroad ties.

My costs for all the materials I had to buy was $8,000.

I developed a water supply from a spring 600 feet above the house and cleared and terraced about an acre of land on the hillside for farming.

Domes

Fate intervened in 1970, after I'd finished the house at Burns Creek. I got into building geodesic domes, and left Big Sur to run a program where we built 17 geodesic domes at an "alternative" (hippie) high school on a 40-acre piece of land in the Santa Cruz mountains over a two-year period. After this, I built my own dome (which was featured in the July 14, 1972 issue of *Life* magazine).

I became disillusioned with domes (as homes) and, after five years of dome research and building and, after having published two books on dome building (including *Domebook* 2), I gave up on domes. It's a long story. If you want more details, you can go to **www.shelterpub.com/domes** for *Refried Domes*, my conclusions on domes.

In 1974, I disassembled and sold my dome and built the house in which we now live *(see p. 2)*. It was a relief to get back to building with vertical walls.

Plywood domes at Pacific High School, 1968–69. Just one problem with the domes: They looked great in photos, but in reality leaked, and had many other things wrong with them.

My last dome. Again, it looked great, but for one thing, covering it with shakes was wasteful in that the shakes had to be cut to fit the ever-tightening circle at the top; also, it was one large room that was hard to subdivide or add on to.

Credits

Book Production: Rick Gordon
Book Design: Lloyd Kahn
Contributing Editor: Lesley Creed
Office Manager: Mary Sangster
Shelter's MacGyver: Evan Kahn
Proofreader: Marianne Rogoff
Printing: Midas Printing Group,
Hong Kong
Printing Consultant: Trevor Shih
Special thanks to Kevin Kelly, who
kept telling me for years that I should
do this book.

Paper:
Text: 128 gsm Gold Sun matt art paper
Cover: 250 GSM 1/S artboard
Press: KBA sheetfed offset press
Production Software: Adobe InDesign,
Adobe Photoshop, Nisus Writer Pro,
BBEdit, AppleScript
Cameras: Olympus OM-D EM-1,
Sony Cyber-shot DSC-RX100 II,
Apple iPhone 6s Plus and 8 Plus
How this book was made:
One way in which this book differs from
all the others we have done is that much
of it, especially photos, was put together
during production.

I'd get to a certain section and realize
I needed photos; I'd grab either my
iPhone 8s or Olympus OM-D EM-1
camera, run out and shoot the photos,
then download them.

Also, as I got to certain subjects, I'd
write text and captions as I was doing layout.

We continue to follow a process where
I do initial layout by printing out photos
(six per sheet of paper), then adjusting
the size on a Brother MFC-9130CW copy
machine. I cut out text with scissors,
then paste down photos, text, headlines,
and pull quotes on layout sheets with
removable Scotch tape. I then mark the
numbers of each photo on these sheets,
gather all of them as well as text in a
folder which I then put into Dropbox, to
which Rick has access from his working
studio at home.

I do the layout two pages at a time,
with no idea how they will all fit together.
During the process, things fall into place.
It's fascinating to watch the book creating
itself day by day.

It's an old-school, new-school process,
where I believe we get the best of both
worlds, as opposed to doing layout on the
computer from the beginning: analog,
then digital.

As we go along, we print out reduced-
size, two-page spreads on plain paper.
I keep these in a pile and continually
shuffle them around, putting them in
what seems like a somewhat logical order.

The next step is that Rick and I go
through all the pages together and make
changes and corrections. At this stage,
the manuscript goes to our proofreader.
Once the proofing corrections are made,
photos or colors are adjusted as necessary,
and we print out full-size proofs on high-
quality proofing paper.

These will be sent to the printer so that
the press operators will see what colors
we want. The entire book is sent electron-
ically to the printers. I have always gone
to the printers to do press checks for color
books on the first printing, but we now
have such good synchronization with
Midas Printing that I haven't felt it
necessary to go to Hong Kong for this one.

The Shelter Library of Building Books

Shelter (1973)

Shelter II (1978)

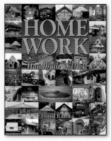

Home Work (2004)

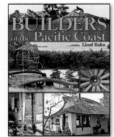

Builders of the Pacific Coast (2008)

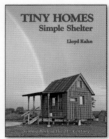

Tiny Homes (2012)

7 books

Over 7,000 photos
of owner-built homes

See the books at:
www.shelterpub.com

Shelter Publications, Inc.

**Celebrating 50 years of publishing
1970–2020**

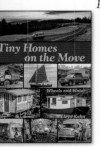

*Tiny Homes on
the Move (2014)*

Small Homes (2017)

Epilogue

It's hard to believe that I wrote the following in our book *Shelter*, 47 years ago, and that it still resonates now in the 21st century:

In times past, people built their own homes, grew their own food, made their own clothes. Knowledge of the building crafts and other skills of providing life's basic needs were generally passed along from father to son, mother to daughter, master to apprentice.

Then, with industrialization and the population shift from country to cities, this knowledge was put aside and much of it has now been lost. We have seen an era of unprecedented prosperity in America based upon huge amounts of foreign and domestic resources and fueled by finite reserves of stored energy.

And as have we have come to realize in recent years, we are running out. Materials are scarce, fuel is in short supply, and prices are escalating. To survive, one is going to have to be either rich or resourceful. Either more dependent upon or free or from central-ized production and controls. The choices are not clear-cut, for these are complex times but it is obvious that the more we can do for ourselves, the greater will our individual freedom and independence be.

This book (Shelter) is not about going off to live in a cave and growing all one's own food. It is not based on the idea that everyone can find an acre in the country, or upon a senti-mental attachment to the past. It is rather about finding a new and necessary balance in our lives between what can be done by hand and what still must be done by machine.

For in times to come, we will have to find a responsive and sensitive balance between the still-usable skills and wisdom of the past and the sustainable products and inventions of the 20th century.

Of necessity, or by choice, there may be a revival of handwork in America. We are certainly capable, and these inherent, dormant talents may prove to be some of our most valuable resources in the future. . . .

Reading this now, 40+ years later, it occurs to me that what we've done, as shown in these pages, is to carry out the main themes of *Shelter*. We've used our hands to create shelter and grow food. We've got a home that we love, and a garden that feeds us, and we've never paid rent nor taken out a mortgage.

Could you do this now, in this digital era? In a world radically transformed from when we started in the '70s? Does it make any sense to hammer and saw, to shovel and rake, to weave and sew — to do stuff by hand — in the mid-21st century?

Well, yes. As our world becomes ever more technological, as housing costs continue to escalate, as the income gap continues to widen, it would seem useful — and vital — to utilize some human skills, even if on a part-time basis.

Pretty much everything you see here was done by hand, and the principles haven't really changed. There's still a use (and need) for using your hands. In fact, in many ways, it now seems more important than ever.